P9-CRZ-885

USS MIDWAY

107

AN ILLUSTRATED GUIDE TO
THE AIR WAR OVER
VIETNAM

Aircraft of the Southeast Asia Conflict

AN ILLUSTRATED GUIDE TO
THE AIR WAR OVER
VIETNAM
Aircraft of the Southeast Asia Conflict

Bernard C. Nalty
George M. Watson Jacob Neufeld

PRENTICE HALL PRESS
New York London Toronto Sydney Tokyo

A Salamander Book

Prentice Hall Press
Gulf + Western Building
One Gulf + Western Plaza
New York, New York 10023

Copyright © 1981 by Salamander
Books Ltd.

An Arco Military Book

Published in 1988 by the Prentice
Hall Trade Division

Originally published in the United
Kingdom by Salamander Books Ltd.

Previously published in the United
States by Arco Publishing, Inc.

PRENTICE HALL PRESS and
colophon are registered trademarks
of Simon & Schuster, Inc.

Library of Congress Catalog
Card Number: 81-67083

ISBN 0-668-05346-1

10 9 8 7 6 5 4 3 2 1

First Prentice Hall Press Edition

Contents

Aircraft are arranged alphabetically by manufacturers' names

The Air War Over Vietnam:

Introduction	6
Bell AH-1 HueyCobra	16
Bell UH-1 Iroquoise	18
Boeing B-52 Stratofortress	22
Boeing KC-135 Stratotanker	28
Boeing-Vertol CH-46 Sea Knight	30
Boeing-Vertol CH-47 Chinook	32
Cessna A-37 Dragonfly	36
Cessna O-1 Bird Dog	38
Cessna O-2	40
de Havilland C-7	42
Douglas A-1 Skyraider	44
Douglas A-26 Invader	48
Douglas C-47	50
Douglas C-133 Cargomaster	54
Douglas C-124 Globemaster II	56
Douglas RB-66 and EA-3B	56
Fairchild C-199 Flying Boxcar	60
Fairchild C-123 Provider	62
General Dynamics F-111	66
Grumman A-6	68
Grumman F8F	70
Grumman HU-16 Albatross	72
Grumman OV-1A	74
Hughes OH-6A Cayuse	76
Kaman HH-43 Huskie	78
Kaman UH-2 SeaSprite	80
Lockheed C-5 Galaxy	82
Lockheed C-130 Hercules	84
Lockheed C-141 StarLifter	90
Lockheed EC-121 Warning Star	92

959.704
N

Credits

Authors: Bernard C. Nalty, Jacob Neufeld and George M. Watson are all historians at the US Office of Air Force History and have contributed to many technical journals on aerospace affairs, official US historical analyses and to technical reference books on US defense affairs, including Salamander's *The Vietnam War: The Illustrated History of the Conflict in Southeast Asia.*

The publishers thank **Bill Gunston** for his invaluable assistance in the preparation of this guide.

Editor: Ray Bonds
Designer: Philip Gorton
Color profiles and line drawings: © Pilot Press Ltd.

Photographs: The publishers wish to thank the official international governmental archives (especially the various US Department of Defense audio-visual agencies), aircraft manufacturers and private collections who have supplied photographs for this book.

Printed in Belgium by Henri Proost et Cie.

Lockheed P-2 Neptune — 94
Lockheed SR-71 — 96
Lockheed U-2 — 98
Lockheed YO-3 — 100
Martin B-57 Canberra — 100
Martin P-5 Marlin — 106
McDonnell Douglas A-4 Skyhawk — 108
McDonnell Douglas F-4 Phantom II — 112
McDonnell RF-101 Voodoo — 118
Mikoyan/Gurevich MiG-17 — 120
Mikoyan/Gurevich MiG-19 — 122
Mikoyan/Gurevich MiG-21 — 122
North American F-100 Super Sabre — 126
North American RA-5 Vigilante — 130
North American T-28 Nomad — 132
North American OV-10 Bronco — 134
Northrop F-5 Freedom Fighter — 136
Republic F-105 Thunderchief — 140
Sikorsky CH-54 — 144
Sikorsky H-34 Choctaw — 146
Sikorsky CH-53 Sea Stallion — 148
Sikorsky HH-3 — 152
Vought A-7 Corsair II — 156
Vought F-8 — 158

158160

The Air War Over Vietnam

THE AIR war over Vietnam involved a wide variety of operations — from air-to-air combat to massive and concentrated aerial bombardment. The aircraft used by the various combatants in a conflict that raged in phases for more than thirty years were also numerous, reaching scores of different types.

This guide sets out to describe and show most of the major types, and to explain how they were used.

The French in Indochina
Long before the Americans arrived in South Vietnam in force, the French were involved in a desperate struggle in the region after World War II, attempting to maintain political control in the face of determined Vietnamese aspirations towards independence, centred on the communist-dominated Viet Minh forces led by Ho Chi Minh and General Vo Nguyen Giap.

For the French, air operations in the early 1950s served exclusively to support the fighting on the ground, attacking Viet Minh troops and supply lines or delivering men and cargo to bases inaccessible by road. The French had hoped for intervention by America, in which case B-29 Superfortresses would probably have attacked not strategic targets (for there were none) but Giap's regiments dug in around Dien Bien Phu where, in May 1954, a French garrison was trapped and facing inevitable annihilation. Intervention never came; the French garrison surrendered, and French forces left the region later that year.

In July 1954 the Geneva Agreements were signed, partitioning Vietnam into North and South along the 17th Parallel. America, attempting to help stem the communist expansion in Southeast Asia, provided assistance directly to South Vietnam (instead of channelling it through the French as previously), and became increasingly drawn into the conflict.

North Vietnamese air power
Following victory at Dien Bien Phu, North Vietnam built an air force with interceptors and a few light bombers. The communist air arm employed its fighters strictly in defense of the North. The skies of South Vietnam remained free of hostile aircraft until shortly before

Below: C-47 of the Armée de l'Air (Indo-Chinoise) AF, with B-26 overhead. Location: Na San, 12 August 1953.

the fall of Saigon in the spring of 1975, and at that time the attacking planes were US-built and flown by South Vietnamese defectors.

Soviet-built MiG fighters formed a major component of North Vietnam's air defense system, along with guns and missiles. The number, location and level of activity of these interceptors varied during the war against the South and American forces. Sometimes the fighters clustered around the main cities of Hanoi and Haiphong; at other times they retreated northward into China to recover from combat losses. In the spring of 1972 North Vietnam's MiG force numbered 200 aircraft, of which 93 were MiG-21s, 33 MiG-19s, and the rest MiG-15s and -17s.

Different types defended the various regions of North Vietnam. The MiG-17 usually opposed carrier strikes in the area by the US Navy. The principal concern of US Seventh Air Force F-4s was the MiG-21, whose pilots, after a sluggish start, began exhibiting greater skill and aggressiveness. Nevertheless, USAF pilots accounted for 137 MiG kills, F-4s claiming 107 victories and F-105s 25.

Support of ground forces

Like their French predecessors, the American authorities considered the ground war decisive, with the fighting in South Vietnam receiving top priority and almost all aerial action designed to contribute to victory there. Three of every four sorties launched from South Vietnamese bases supported ground forces in any of several ways.

Strikes in close proximity to embattled troops were comparatively few, but there were countless ▶

Right: In 1968 there were more than 90 tac airfields in South Vietnam, most poor.

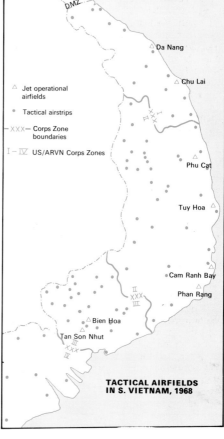

Jet operational airfields

Tactical airstrips

×××— Corps Zone boundaries

I – IV US/ARVN Corps Zones

DMZ

Da Nang

Chu Lai

Phu Cat

Tuy Hoa

Cam Ranh Bay

Phan Rang

Bien Hoa

Tan Son Nhut

TACTICAL AIRFIELDS IN S. VIETNAM, 1968

▶thousands of airlift sorties, armed reconnaissance or interdiction missions, and sorties devoted to tactical reconnaissance, battlefield illumination, and the spraying of herbicide and pesticide. B-52 Stratofortresses, basic elements in America's strategic deterrence and designed for nuclear war, were used for more than seven years in what was essentially a tactical role, dropping millions of pounds of so-called iron bombs, or non-nuclear ordnance, in support of ground forces. They served as flying artillery, battering enemy supply dumps, troop concentrations, and supply lines far from the battlefield.

Conversely, for a time, American airmen used tactical aircraft in the hope of achieving a strategic purpose. President Lyndon B. Johnson and his advisers seemed to believe that fighter-bombers could exert a pressure that would persuade Ho Chi Minh and his communist colleagues to abandon their plan to overrun the South. When strategic persuasion failed, the United States shifted to aerial interdiction.

Lines of supply and communications became the principal targets, as bombing restrictions shifted the focus of the air war from all of North Vietnam to the panhandle region and to southern Laos. Supply depots and base camps in Cambodia came under attack, first secretly by B-52s and then by tactical and ground troops. But even then interdiction could not succeed; the enemy retained the initiative and adjusted the level of combat to the available manpower and munitions.

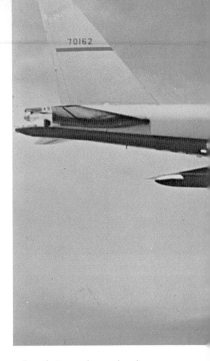

US bombing successes

Not until 1972 did aerial interdiction become a decisive factor. In the spring of that year, the enemy launched a conventional invasion that depended for momentum upon a steady flow of reinforcements and supplies. War materiel had to enter the North over the rail line from China or through Haiphong and the other ports, and then move southward to the battlefront. North Vietnam had gambled, committing itself to sustaining a ground campaign that was becoming increasingly costly in lives, munitions, and equipment.

By cutting the main rail line and mining the ports, US air power choked the flow of supplies so that what was expended could not be replaced. When the B-52s attacked Hanoi and Haiphong in December 1972, they therefore achieved a multiple effect. This was the B-52's most spectacular achievement, the so-called "Eleven Day War", in which, besides disrupting the distribution of supplies on hand and lowering civilian morale, the raids forced the enemy to expend a hoard of missiles and shells that could not be replaced.

Although costly to the US in terms of aircraft and crews lost, the campaign proved decisive. It drove the communists to the peace table where North Vietnam had little choice but to agree to a ceasefire. It was a respite during which, in 1973, American forces left South Vietnam, and both the communist regime and its rival in the South could gird for the eventual renewal of violence, which came in the spring of 1975 and ended in a North Vietnamese victory.

Above: The standard bomb truck of the US Air Force in the Vietnam War was the Boeing B-52. Ultimately the chief model was the B-52D, with "Big Belly" rebuild, but this is a B-52F.

Fighters and attack aircraft

From 1965 until late 1968 and again in 1972, the critical battle-ground for the air war in Southeast Asia was North Vietnam. When attacking the North, American airmen faced a modern radar-directed air defense network patterned on a Soviet model. But, at the time of the 1964 strikes in retaliation for the Tonkin Gulf incident (when US destroyers were apparently attacked by North Vietnamese torpedo boats), North Vietnam's defenses consisted mainly of optically aimed automatic weapons and light anti-aircraft guns.

As late as the spring of 1965, a series of sustained aerial attacks might have crippled the air defenses, at least temporarily, but the Johnson administration was reluctant to escalate the war and risk inflicting severe casualties on the civilian populace.

Detailed rules of engagement governed the air war. For a time surface-to-air missile sites could not be bombed; during other periods, airfields used by MiG fighters were immune to attack, as were targets deemed too close to Hanoi and Haiphong. No wonder that US airmen complained that they had to fly with one eye reading the rules and the other looking for the enemy.

After 1966 US Air Force planners adopted the fighter sweep, reasoning that, since the rules of engagement placed enemy airfields out of bounds, the MiGs would have to be lured into battle. This gambit sometimes involved a pincer action in which American fighters approaching from the east tried to cut off MiGs seeking safety over China after intercepting a strike that had come from the west.

Reconnaissance and electronic warfare

Aerial reconnaissance, whether by the supersonic SR-71A or the slow-flying C-47D, was essential to the conduct of America's Southeast Asia war. As against the

French, the enemy moved through narrow valleys over roads and trails concealed by the jungle canopy, suddenly materialized, and attacked. South Vietnam's defenders lacked the manpower to seal the nation's porous borders against infiltration.

In place of men, the United States turned to machines—aircraft, cameras, and a variety of sensors—and the enemy adopted crude but effective countermeasures.

Throughout the conflict, the North Vietnamese and Viet Cong tried to hide their movement, concentrations, and intentions, while the Americans sought to penetrate the curtain of darkness and greenery.

Like most other aspects of the Southeast Asia conflict, aerial reconnaissance began on a limited scale and expanded rapidly. In the earliest missions, a camera-equipped C-47D was used to

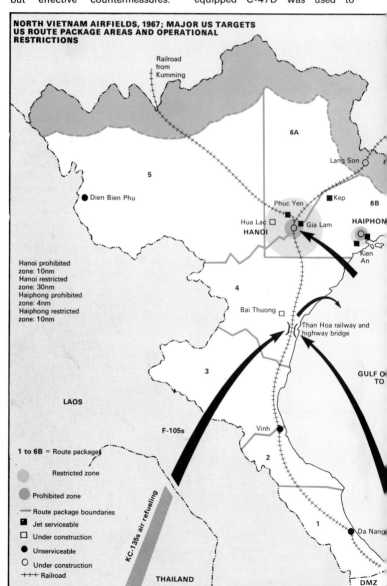

NORTH VIETNAM AIRFIELDS, 1967; MAJOR US TARGETS
US ROUTE PACKAGE AREAS AND OPERATIONAL
RESTRICTIONS

Railroad from Kumming

6A

Lang Son

5

Dien Bien Phu

Phuc Yen

Kep

6B

Hua Lac

Gia Lam

HAIPHON

HANOI

Kien An

Hanoi prohibited zone: 10nm
Hanoi restricted zone: 30nm
Haiphong prohibited zone: 4nm
Haiphong restricted zone: 10nm

4

Bai Thuong

Than Hoa railway and highway bridge

3

GULF O TO

LAOS

F-105s

Vinh

1 to 6B = Route packages

Restricted zone

Prohibited zone

Route package boundaries

■ Jet serviceable

□ Under construction

● Unserviceable

○ Under construction

+++ Railroad

2

1

Da Nang

KC-135s air refueling

THAILAND

DMZ

photograph communist disposi-
tions in Laos during the early
months of 1961, until fire from
automatic weapons downed it.

The jet-propelled Lockheed
RT-33 was next on the scene,
followed by the RF-101C Voodoo,
which eventually operated from
both South Vietnam and Thailand.
The RB-26C, the type used by the
French earlier, also saw action.

Except for the RF-101C, most of
the tactical reconnaissance aircraft
were approaching obsolescence.
Once the air war began in earnest,
an armada of modern planes joined
the Voodoo—the Air Force RF-4C
and the Navy's RF-8 and RA-5C,
supplementing the high-altitude
efforts of the U-2 and SR-71.

Specialized sensors

To thwart the aerial camera, the
North Vietnamese and Viet Cong
habitually moved at night, keeping
beneath the jungle canopy if
possible. To find an elusive foe,
airmen used a variety of sensors,
some of them installed on standard
reconnaissance aircraft, others
mounted on specialized types like
flareships, gunships, observation
planes, and even helicopters.

Infrared detectors, pioneered by
the RB-57E, could locate heat
sources such as campfires in hidden
bivouac areas—or decoy blazes set
by the enemy—and infrared film
recorded heat variations like those
caused by the exhaust from a truck
convoy driving through the night.
Image intensifiers, low-light-level
television and radar proved valuable, and perhaps the most unusual
device of all was a "people sniffer"
that reacted to the scent of the
human body. ▶

CHINA

Railroad
from
Nanning

Left: American crews
in the Vietnam war
were hamstrung by a
long list of political
rules and restrictions,
which as this map
shows also extended
to where they were
permitted to fly.

Below: Though the
the same manu-
facturer's RF-4C was
becoming available,
the chief dedicated
USAF reconnaissance
aircraft at the start
of the war was the
RF-101C, one of
which is seen here on
a combat mission in
May 1967.

▶ Electronic warfare

A few camera-equipped RB-66s flew reconnaissance missions over South Vietnam, but most planes of this type engaged in electronic warfare, both jamming radar and analysing the signal itself. Indeed, electronic countermeasures proved essential in the air war against heavily defended parts of North Vietnam.

To make up for the limitations imposed—and to compensate for a tendency toward stereo-typed tactics—the attackers came to rely on electronic countermeasures to frustrate North Vietnamese radar. Standoff jamming by planes like the Navy EA-1F, the Marine Corps EF-10B, and the Air Force EB-66B or E proved inadequate and was supplemented by jamming pods mounted on the individual fighter-bombers. Clouds or corridors of radar-reflecting chaff also helped to protect strike forces, especially during the 1972 fighting.

The key weapon against the surface-to-air missile was Wild Weasel, a two-place fighter-bomber modified to locate the radar-acquiring targets for this weapon and then destroy the transmitter or force it to shut down by launching a radar-homing missile.

Almost as important as jamming was radar control from either ground stations or from orbiting EC-121 Constellations. These circled to warn of North Vietnamese fighter attack, or directed American planes into position to destroy MiGs—missions that had evolved from the plane's earlier surveillance role, guarding against aerial incursions from the North and warning of possible violation of Chinese airspace.

Ironically, the primitive battle-fields of Southeast Asia pulsated with electronic armaments. In this environment, adaptability became the order of the day and doctrine, tactics and weapons designed for other forms of warfare were shed or modified to meet the needs of the Vietnam War.

Observation planes

Especially in areas where there was a danger of bombing either friendly troops or potentially friendly non-combatants, a critical role was played by observation planes. The US Air Force assigned the aircraft to forward air controllers who operated from advance airstrips in support of major ground units, locating targets for air and artillery strikes, conducting last-minute reconnaissance, and linking the rifleman with the pilot supporting him.

These forward air controllers, called airborne controllers by the

Below: Air Force personnel loading Acoubuoy (Igloo White) sensors into an aft-firing SUU-42/A dispenser.

Below: At the start the chief light FAC (forward air control) aircraft was the Cessna O-1E Bird Dog.

US Marine Corps, formed part of a centralized control mechanism that, after March 1968, included Marine as well as Air Force fighter, attack and tactical reconnaissance squadrons. The strike aircraft that checked in with a forward air controller could be responding to an immediate request: a ground commander called for help, and the nearest direct air support center responded to the emergency, usually by diverting a plane already in the air on some less critical mission, although sometimes by sending an aircraft which was on airborne alert or standing by at an air base.

Transport aircraft

Among the functions of air power is airlift, both world-wide and within the combat theater. During the Southeast Asia conflict the United States used strategic air lift as long-range transports, supplemented by chartered airliners, flew men and cargo across the Pacific. Older planes like the piston-engined C-118 and C-124A, and the turbo-prop C-133A and B, gradually gave way to more modern jets such as the C-141A and massive C-5A.

Within South Vietnam, American advisers at first substituted the Air Force C-123B and Army CV-2 for truck convoys that could not travel over roads menaced by the communist Viet Cong. Besides carrying troops or military cargo, these

Above: An AC-130H, biggest and most powerful of the gunships.

planes sometimes delivered pigs, chickens or other foodstuffs for the inhabitants of isolated villages.

Even though ground forces re-opened many of the highways, a centralized airlift network, operated by the US Air Force, enabled ground commanders to supply, reinforce, or evacuate isolated outposts and rapidly shift troops through the country. Frequently, the plane that landed men and equipment at a combat base took off within minutes with a load of wounded.

Transports often braved enemy fire to land at besieged outposts or used panels laid out on the ground as markers in parachuting supplies to troops below, and the C-123s and C-130s dropped South Vietnamese airborne forces.

The most versatile of the transports used was the C-130 Hercules, which could, for instance, para-chute cargo containers from altitudes beyond the range of light anti-aircraft guns, the crews releasing the load upon order from radar operators on the ground. Items too bulky to be para dropped were deployed from the open cargo hatch by a parachute that snatched the load from the plane which was flying a few feet above the ground, or sometimes the pilot might fly so ▶

▶ low, almost touching down, that a trailing hook could engage an arresting cable rigged across the runway and pull the heavily laden pallet from the aircraft.

In addition to carrying out these primary missions, transports dispensed flares to illuminate targets for other aircraft or for infantrymen below, released chemicals to create mud or rain, conducted reconnaissance, served as airborne command posts for strike or rescue efforts, refueled other aircraft, sprayed insecticides or herbicides and, in the case of the C-130 and a variant of the C-123, dropped high explosives.

Aerial refueling

Aerial tankers played an important role, not only for B-52s flying the 5,500 miles (8850km) round trip out of Guam but also for fighter-bombers based in South Vietnam or Thailand. The hot, humid air of South Vietnam reduced lift and increased the takeoff distance for most aircraft. Had it not been for the tankers, mission planners would have had to sacrifice bombs for fuel in order to avoid exceeding the maximum takeoff weight, while still making sure that the plane could reach its target and return.

Helicopter operations

Besides its reconnaissance and transport functions, the helicopter acquired a new role during the Vietnam War. It became a weapons platform, a gunship that could seek out and destroy enemy targets.

A bold and imaginative development, the concept of the helicopter-borne assault appealed to the American military tactician because it enabled him to shift forces rapidly and on short notice. Under the US Army's airmobility concept, aircraft assumed the role of light mechanized columns—in hit-and-run raids and armed reconnaissance operations. It did not take long before the term "sky cavalry" gained general acceptance in describing heli-borne operations.

The US Army emphasized airmobility as a means of meeting the threat of limited war throughout the world. Generally, the idea was to replace many of the ground vehicles

—trucks, jeeps, and weapons carriers—by helicopters, or other slow-flying aircraft capable of operating out of small airstrips and clearings.

The Vietnam War witnessed the swift development of airmobility as reliance on helicopters grew steadily. By January 1966 the United States had deployed about 1,000 helicopters into the war zone. Of these, 428 belonged to one unit, the First Cavalry Division (Airmobile), which had specifically planned around the concept of helicopter mobility. Dubbed the "Flying Horsemen", the 16,000-man division arrived in Vietnam in August 1965, with the UH-1 and CH-47A, both turbine-powered helicopters, as its mainstays.

A little over two years later, the AH-1 HueyCobra arrived on the scene, as an armed escort and to provide fire support for the CH-47. It was not long before it saw action, being used in a suppression strike against Viet Cong bands pinning down the Air Force's 3rd Security Squadron at Bien Hoa Air base, during the nationwide communist Tet Offensive. Time and again the HueyCobras swept into the VC area, flying just feet off the ground and in the face of heavy

fire directed at them. The helicopter actions were reported to have been the turning point in the enemy's destruction.

Casualty evacuation

The helicopter also made a significant contribution to casualty evacuation in Southeast Asia. Nearly all US and South Vietnamese Army battlefield casualties were "helilifted" to rear areas for emergency treatment. US Air Force transports then evacuated patients needing major medical attention to facilities elsewhere in Southeast Asia, or to the United States.

The helicopter had other effects on military medicine, too. Mobile surgical hospitals no longer needed to be so mobile, nor so numerous. Instead of moving the hospital to keep it close to the scene of a battle, the helicopter could move casualties swiftly over longer distances.

Below: Urgently produced by Bell Helicopter Textron as an interim machine to replace the AH-56A Cheyenne, the AH-1 HueyCobra became one of the successes of US defense procurement. This was one of the first AH-1G Cobras to arrive in South Vietnam in 1967.

Utility planes and patrol aircraft

Utility planes served all combatants in the war, performing a wide variety of duties. The aircraft carried important passengers, delivered parcels to isolated outposts, conducted reconnaissance and, in the case of the Cessna U-17s given the South Vietnamese, served as vehicles for forward air controllers.

The French Air Force more or less established the pattern for employing these versatile aircraft. After all, the Morane-Saulnier Cricket, which had folded wings for easy storage in hastily-built revetments, was a flying ambulance, courier plane, and artillery observation craft.

Also useful as a light transport, the HU-16B Albatross bridged the gap between utility and patrol craft, spending hours on station over the Tonkin Gulf while carrying out its mission as rescue craft. Patrol planes like the P-2 and SP-5 also made long over-water flights, but these searched for North Vietnamese junks attempting to smuggle arms and ammunition to forces in South Vietnam, and kept watch for possible intervention by Chinese or Soviet submarines.

Bell AH-1 HueyCobra

AH-1G, AH-1J.

Origin: Bell Helicopter Company.
Type: Single-rotor armed helicopter.
Engines: One 1,400shp Lycoming T53-L-13 turboshaft.
Dimensions: Main rotor (two-blade) diameter 44ft (13·41m); fuselage length 44ft 5in (13·54m); overall height 13ft $7\frac{1}{4}$in (4·14m).
Weight: Operating 6,073lb (2754kg); maximum takeoff and landing 9,500lb (4309kg); payload 1,993lb (905kg).
Performance: Maximum speed (at maximum takeoff weight) 219mph (352km/h); range 357 miles (574km) at sea level, with maximum fuel and with eight percent reserve.
Armament: GAU-2B/A (formerly XM-134) minigun six-barrel 7·62mm machinegun with 8,000 rounds; superseded by the XM-28 subsystem which mounted either two miniguns of 4,000 rounds each, two 40mm grenade launchers with 300 rounds each, or one minigun and one grenade launcher. Also carried external stores under the stub wings, such as, 76 2·75in rockets.
Accommodation: Two crew.
History: First flight 7 September 1965. A development of the UH-1B/C Iroquois. On 11 March 1966 the US Army announced its intention to order production models. First delivery in 1967. Initial production numbered 110 aircraft. By October 1968 there were 838 productions. On 30 January 1970 another 170 aircraft were ordered and 70 more placed in mid-1970.
Users: US Army (AH-1G), US Marine Corps (AH-1J).

Tactical employment: The HueyCobra came into being as the result of a crash program initiated by US Army when the Vietnam War revealed the need for a fast, well-armed helicopter to provide escort and fire support for the CH-47A Chinook. None of the existing helicopters in the Army inventory possessed the speed, endurance and firepower to accomplish the job.

From initial orders in April 1966, the Army had ordered 838 AH-1Gs by the spring of 1968. It first became operational in Vietnam in November 1967. In May 1968 the US Marine Corps ordered 49 of the craft under the designation AH-1J.

The "Cobra," which replaced the UH-1C, had more speed, better armor, and better armaments than its predecessor. The first six HueyCobras arrived in South Vietnam in September 1967 and were assigned to the New Equipment Training Team, 1st Aviation Brigade. The training team travelled to various helicopter units to standardize procedures and to identify operational and maintenance problems.

Right: AH-1 HueyCobra "Canned Heat" of 20th "Blue Max" Aerial Rocket Artillery, US Army, Vietnam.

Three-view of Bell AH-1G (or similar T53-powered model).

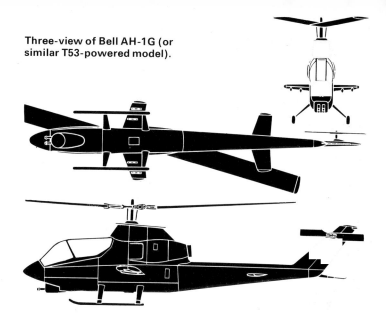

During 1970 and 1971, Cobra gunships demonstrated both their ability to attack accurately enemy positions, and to absorb punishment. In the Cambodian and the combined operation into Laos, Cobras used rockets and machine guns to disperse enemy formations and (in 1971) to kill enemy PT-76 tanks, often operating under low-ceiling weather conditions. Although many were hit by 12·7mm fire, the Cobras returned to base and eventually re-entered combat.

Above: Army and Marine Corps pilots soon had the skill and courage to take Cobras into very hazardous places.

Bell UH-1 Iroquois

UH-1B, UH-1D, UH-1H.

Origin: Bell Helicopter Company.
Type: Single-rotor general purpose helicopter.
Engines: (UH-1H) One 1,400shp Lycoming T53-L-13 turboshaft.
Dimensions: (UH-1H) Main rotor (two-blade) diameter 48ft (14·63m); fuselage length 41ft 1in (12·77m).
Weight: (UH-1H) Empty 4,667lb (2116kg); basic operating (troop carrier mission) 2,557lb (2520kg); maximum takeoff and landing 9,500lb (4309kg).
Performance: (UH-1H) Maximum speed (at maximum takeoff weight) 127mph (204km/h); range 318 miles (511km).
Armament: (UH-1B) Four M-60 machine guns 7·62mm; grenade launcher 40mm; 48 2·75in rockets; M 22 guided missile.
Accommodation: Two pilots, 11 to 14 troops, or 6 litters and a medical attendant, or 3,880lb (1759kg) of freight.
History: First YUH-1D flight on 16 August 1961. First delivered to US Army on 9 August 1963; 319 UH-1H initially delivered; in 1971 300 more ordered and additional 500 ordered by 1973.
User: US Army.

Tactical employment: Nicknamed "Huey", the UH-1B first arrived in Vietnam in November 1962. More than any other type, the UH-1 was the workhorse of the Vietnam War, where it was used for a wide variety of roles, including troop transport, armed patrol, and escort. The UH-1D was the most numerous version with nearly 3,000 helicopters ordered by the end of 1966. The UH-1H is identical to the D model except for the T53-L-13 engine. In the spring of 1968, 576 of the H model were ordered. Beginning in mid-1966, large numbers of the UH-1 have been refitted with Decca navigation equipment and lightweight armored crew seats. ▶

Left: US Navy SEAL (Sea/Air/Land) combat team abseiling down to set up a jungle ambush in 1967. The Huey was used almost exclusively for this.

Right: Putting down combat troops where no landing was possible.

Right: Most numerous of all variants, the UH-1D introduced a stretched cabin.

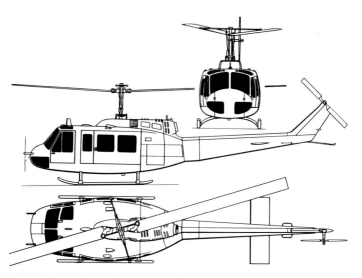

Above: Three-view of an advanced model, the UH-1N.

▶   Although any helicopter could carry wounded from the battlefield, the US Army left nothing to chance, forming specialized helicopter ambulance units. At the peak of American involvement there were 116 UH-1 helicopter ambulances in service, fitted to carry six litter patients. Each US division had a medical battalion and most of these had helicopter ambulances assigned. Their task was to evacuate battle casualties to a medical clearing station from where non-divisional helicopters moved the patients to a field hospital. In some situations the helicopters could not land. They would then lower a spring-loaded hoist and hover until the wounded soldier or pilot was retrieved. While hovering, the helicopter made an inviting target for enemy fire. During 1968 35 helicopters were hit and and 39 were hit in 1969. However, thousands of casualties were rescued in this manner. The alternative would have been to carry the wounded to a site where a landing could be made, but with consequent delay in medical care. Crewed by two pilots, a flight crewman and a medical aideman, the Huey provided timely medical emergency support. Between 1965 and 1969 a total of 372,947 casualties were evacuated by helicopter (this figure includes US personnel, ARVN and other friendly troops and civilians).

Right: This photograph of a crew member firing an M60 from a UH-1H gives an idea of the Huey cabin volume of 220 cubic feet.

Below right: Troops of the USA 1st Cavalry Division (Airmobile) jump from a UH-1D during Operation Oregon, a "search and destroy" operation, in the earlier part of the war in April 1967.

Below: Airlifting Vietnam Marines in the Mekong delta region.

Boeing B-52 Stratofortress

B-52D, F, G – data for -D.

Origin: Boeing Airplane Company.
Type: Strategic heavy bomber.
Engines: Eight 13,750lb Pratt and Whitney J-57-P-19W, -29WA.
Dimensions: Span 185ft (56·33m); length 156ft 6in (47·70m).
Weights: Empty 177,816lb (80,728kg); combat 293,100lb (133,117kg); takeoff 450,000lb (204,300kg).
Performance: Maximum speed at 20,200ft (6156m) 551kts; combat radius 3,012nm (5581km).
Flight crew: Six.
Armament: Four 50-cal M-3 guns; bombload of approximately 60,000lb (27,240kg).
History: First flight YB-52 prototype 15 April 1952; (B-52D) 4 June 1956; (B-52F) 6 May 1958.
User: US Air Force, Strategic Air Command.

Tactical employment: In February 1965 the Strategic Air Command (SAC) deployed two B-52F squadrons to Andersen Air Force Base, Guam, for possible use over South Vietnam. On 18 June the B-52s saw their first action of the Vietnam conflict flying from Guam to strike a suspected communist troop base area in Binh Duong province north of Saigon. Although unsuccessful, the operation marked the beginning of the extensive use of the B-52 which was code named Arc Light.

Commander of the United States Military Assistance Command, Vietnam, General William Westmoreland, considered the B-52 so vital that he

Above: The B-52D and F force had black sides and undersurfaces.

"personally dealt with requests [for B-52 strikes] from field commanders, reviewed the targets, and normally allocated the available bomber resources on a daily basis".

In December 1965 the US Air Force initiated a special modification program to enable the B-52D to carry additional bombs. Known as the Big Belly modification, the program left the outside of the aircraft intact. Externally, the strategic bomber could still carry either 24 500lb (227kg) bombs or 750lb (340kg) bombs, but its internal bombload was increased to about 60,000lb (27,240kg), 22,000lb (9988kg) more than the B-52F. ▶

Below: Smoking in water-injection power, a B-52D thunders off the switchback runway at Guam with empty pylons.

▶ In April 1966 the D models of SAC's 28th and 484th Bombardment Wings deployed to Guam to replace the B-52Fs. In the spring of 1967 the B-52Ds also began to operate out of U Tapao, Thailand, from where they could operate without needing inflight refueling.

About June 1966 two actions were taken to enhance further the B-52's flexibility of operations. The first involved the introduction of the Combat Skyspot bombing system, whereby ground radar units directed the bombers over enemy targets and indicated the exact moment of bomb release. The second innovation was the creation of a six-aircraft alert force standing by on Guam to respond to battlefield emergencies. A highlight of the 1966 campaign was the defeat of the Viet Cong 9th Division. B-52s flew 225 sorties in support of this action. During the second year of the buildup of United States forces in Vietnam the B-52s participated in several major actions, such as the Battle of Dak To, where the Stratofortresses flew some 2,000 sorties.

Above: Millions of dollars went into taxiways and hardstands at Andersen AFB, Guam, for the B-52s and supporting KC-135 tankers.

Left: Each external pylon carried a normal load of four triplets of 750lb or 1,000lb bombs. These are fuzed, ready for takeoff.

From a rate of approximately 300 sorties each month late in 1965, the B-52 effort gradually increased to 800 sorties during 1967 and for the first two weeks of February 1968 rose to 1,200 sorties. On 15 February General Westmoreland was authorized to increase the number to 1,800 and to use the B-52 force based at Kadena, Okinawa. Viewed initially as temporary, this rate remained in effect until 1969 when it was cut back to 1,600 sorties.

During the Battle for Khe Sanh, from January through March 1968, some 2,700 B-52 sorties dropped 110,000 tons of ordnance. A three-plane B-52 cell arrived every 90 minutes during the height of the battle. They destroyed enemy bunkers and supplies, exploded his ammunition, and caved in his tunnels near the Khe Sahn perimeter. It was reported that 75 percent of one 1,800-man enemy regiment had been killed by a single B-52 strike.

The B-52 made its debut over North Vietnam in April 1966 with a strike near the Mu Gia Pass through which men and supplies moved through Laos into South Vietnam. Until the North Vietnamese 1972 offensive, B-52s rarely attacked the North, instead attacking in South Vietnam, Cambodia, and Laos, none as heavily defended as the Hanoi-Haiphong corridor. Each B-52 mission was flown against communist lines of communications leading through the demilitarized zone (DMZ), and against the Ho Chi Minh Trail in Laos each mission normally dropped between 25 and 30 tons of bombs.

In December 1968 a number of B-52Ds underwent yet another modification program. This time the purpose was to permit the aircraft to carry aerial mines. Completed in the fall of 1971, this change paid off in May 1972 when President Richard M. Nixon ordered the mining of North Vietnam's harbors and river inlets.

When the North Vietnamese launched an attack across the DMZ in March 1972, the US responded with heavy B-52 strikes. But these were only a prelude of a much larger action begun on 18 December 1972. Called Linebacker II, 740 B-52D and B-52G aircraft sorties were launched in a massive attack against the previously restricted targets in the Hanoi-Haiphong area. Except for a 24-hour Christmas respite, the bombing lasted ▶

▶ until 29 December. The targets included rail yards, power plants, communications facilities, air defense radars, docks and shipping facilities, POL stores, and ammunition supply dumps. The bombers also hit the principal MiG bases of the North Vietnamese Air Force. The enemy responded by loosing nearly its entire supply of 1,000 surface-to-air missiles (SAMs) and a devastating barrage of anti-aircraft artillery. Fifteen B-52s were shot down and three damaged. However, the enemy defenses were battered and his supply of missiles all but exhausted, so that on the last two days of Linebacker II the B-52s flew over Hanoi and Haiphong without suffering any damage. During the campaign the North Vietnamese could muster only 32 aircraft against the attackers, and eight of the 32 were shot down. Two of these were downed by B-52 tail gunners.

On 18 December Staff Sergeant Samuel O. Turner was the tail gunner aboard a B-52D attacking Hanoi when he picked up an enemy fighter on his radar scope. Turner squeezed off a short burst and shot down what was later confirmed as a MiG-21. On 24 December Airman First Class Albert E. Moore, a B-52 tail gunner, on a mission against the Thai Nguyen railyards, picked up a fast moving target on his radar scope. When the object, later confirmed as a MiG-21, came within 2,000 yards (1828m), Moore opened fire and continued shooting until the blip disappeared from the screen.

On 30 December President Nixon announced the resumption of peace talks with the North Vietnamese in Paris and an agreement was subsequently signed on 23 January 1973.

Between 1968 and 1972 only 9,800 sorties were flown against the North. The B-52s dropped approximately 110,000 tons of ordnance. In the campaign against the Cambodian sanctuaries, from 18 March 1969 to 26 May 1970 the B-52s flew 4,308 sorties delivering 120,578 tons of bombs.

From June 1965 to August 1973 no fewer than 126,615 B-52 sorties were launched. Of these, 125,479 reached their targets and 124,532 dropped their bombs. Geographically, 55 percent of the sorties were flown against targets in South Vietnam, 27 percent in Laos, 12 percent in Cambodia, and 6 percent in North Vietnam. Altogether, Strategic Air Command lost 29 B-52s, 17 to hostile fire (all over the North) and 12 from other causes.

Right: Rear defense system of the B-52D was the Bosch Arma MD-9A tail turret with four 0·5in (12·7mm) guns, and with the gunner in a pressurized tail cockpit facing aft. Here the fairings are off for maintenance and the ammunition feeds can be seen.

Below: 750lb bombs are dropped while checking out the new underwing pylons with a B-52F. Note the white sides and black under-surface.

Boeing KC-135 Stratotanker

KC-135A, C-135A, B Stratolifter.

Origin: The Boeing Company.
Type: Tanker (KC-135A), transport (C-135A, B).
Engines: (KC-135A, C-135A) four 13,750lb (6240kg) thrust Pratt & Whitney J57-P-59W turbojets; (C-135B) 18,000lb (8165kg) thrust Pratt & Whitney TF33-P-5 turbofans.
Dimensions: Span 130ft 10in (39·88m); length (KC-135A) 136ft 3in (49·05m), (C-135A, B) 134ft 6in (48·42m); height (KC-135A and first three C-135As) 38ft 4in (11·5m); (all others) 41ft 7in (12·47m).
Weight: (KC-135A) empty 98,466lb (44,310kg); gross weight 297,000lb (133,650kg); (C-135A) normal takeoff weight 272,000lb (123,375kg); (C-135B) normal takeoff weight 275,000lb (123,975kg).
Performance: (KC-135A) maximum speed 600mph (965km/h); cruising speed 552mph (883·2km/h); range 3,000 miles (4800km); (C-135A) maximum speed 600mph (965km/h), cruising speed 530mph (850km/h), range 4,000 miles (6400km); (C-135B) maximum speed 604mph (966·4km/h); range 4,625 miles (7445km).
Armament: None.
Flight crew: Three to five.
History: (KC-135A) first flight 31 August 1956; (C-135A) the first of three prototypes converted from KC-135As flew on 19 May 1961; (C-135B) first flight 15 February 1962, with the first deliveries during that same month.
Users: US Air Force Strategic Air Command (KC-135A), Military Airlift Command (C-135A, B).

Tactical employment: The KC-135A, fitted with internal tanks and an extendable boom for transferring fuel while in flight, evolved from the Boeing 367-80 jet transport prototype, first flown in July 1954. The Strato-tanker carried a total of 31,200 US gallons of fuel for both consumption in its own engines and transfer to other aircraft at a rate as rapid as 1,000 US gallons per minute. During refueling, a boom operator at the rear of the tanker steered the nozzle into a receptacle on the other aircraft, which maintained a position below and behind the tanker.

Below: A KC-135A about to contact an F-105D; compared with the commercial 707 the KC has a smaller airframe and J57 turbojets.

Above: Another photograph from the same F-105D refuelling sortie; the star-spangled band is that of the parent command, SAC.

In Southeast Asia, the KC-135A performed its first refueling mission in June 1964, when four of the Stratotankers transferred fuel to eight F-100Ds en route to attack communist anti-aircraft batteries in northern Laos. Refueling operations expanded to keep pace with the tempo of the air war, peaking during Operation Rolling Thunder, the bombing of North Vietnam, then declining after President Lyndon Johnson ended that campaign. The KC-135A remained active, however, during Commando Hunt, the sustained effort to impede the passage of North Vietnamese troops and supplies through southern Laos. The year 1972, which saw a resumption of the bombing of the North, produced even greater activity than 1968, previously the most hectic period, as a reinforced tanker fleet flew almost 35,000 sorties. Throughout the Southeast Asia air war, which ended in August 1973 with the final strikes in Cambodia, the KC-135As flew almost 200,000 sorties, conducted more than 800,000 refuelings, and transferred almost 9 billion pounds (4.1 billion kilograms) of fuel.

The Stratotankers, moreover, were available in case of emergency. Aircraft low on fuel could replenish their supply in order to reach their base or the aircraft carrier that had launched them. Indeed, a KC-135A might on occasion refuel US Air Force and Navy planes in rapid succession.

The Stratotanker performed missions other than refueling. The A model, for instance, could carry 80 troops on a deck above the fuel storage tanks. The KC-135B, not flown in Southeast Asia, obtained improved performance from turbofan engines and, while retaining its refueling boom, served as an airborne command post using elaborate communications gear.

The first transport versions, the turbojet C-135A and turbofan C-135B, represented a stopgap solution to the need for a long-range jet transport, pending the appearance of the C-141A. Until the StarLifter made its debut, the C-135 Stratolifters maintained regular service to South Vietnam, flying as many as 126 passengers westward and returning with as many as 98 wounded, 54 seated and 44 on litters. Although capable of delivering a $2\frac{1}{2}$-day supply of small-arms ammunition for an airborne division, the Stratolifter could not carry the kind of bulky cargo for which the C-141A and C-5A were being designed. The combination of side-loading and a comparatively narrow cargo compartment imposed limitations on the plane's capacity.

Like most other transports, the C-135 performed a variety of activities in Southeast Asia. Reconnaissance versions flew missions in the area, and a lavishly appointed variant, the VC-137, a much larger and heavier aircraft based on the 707-320, flew government officials, including President Richard M. Nixon, to South Vietnam.

Boeing-Vertol CH-46 Sea Knight

CH-46A.

Origin: Boeing Vertol Company.
Type: Twin-engined medium transport and assault helicopter.
Engines: Two 1,250shp General Electric T58-GE-8B turboshaft.
Dimensions: Tandem main (3-blade) rotor diameter 50ft (15·24m); fuselage length 44ft 10in (13·66m); overall height 16ft 8½in (5·09m).
Weight: Empty 12,400lb (5627kg); maximum takeoff and landing 23,000lb (10,433kg).
Performance: Maximum speed 166mph (267km/h); range at maximum weight with 6,750lb (3062kg) payload plus ten percent reserve 236 miles (380km).
Armament: None.
Accommodation: Three crew, 17 to 25 troops, or 15 litters and two attendants or 4,000lb (1814kg) of cargo.
History: (Model 107) first flight 22 April 1958; (CH-46A) first flight 16 October 1962.
Users: US Marine Corps and US Navy.

Tactical employment: The US Army considered the CH-46 too heavy for the assault role and too light for the transport role. It decided, therefore, to upgrade the more maneuverable UH-1 Huey as a tactical troop transport and to procure a heavy transport helicopter. The Marines, however, stayed with the Sea Knight which supplied Marines manning hilltop outposts during the fight for Khe Sanh.

Above: A CH-46D dropping supplies to K Company, 1st Marine Division, during Operation Upshur Stream in early February 1971.

Right: CH-46D Sea Knights of the Marine Corps take off in 1971 on an air/ground support mission.

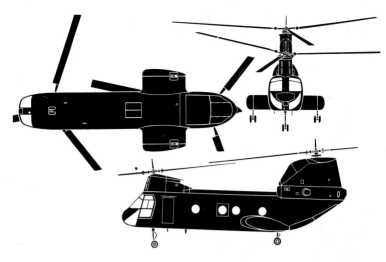

Above: Three-view of CH-46 (all variants basically similar).

Above: This Marine Corps CH-46D was photographed in 1966 disembarking Marines from LPH-5 USS *Princeton*.

Boeing-Vertol CH-47 Chinook

CH-47C.

Origin: Boeing Vertol Company.
Type: Twin-engined medium transport helicopter.
Engines: Two 3,750shp Lycoming T55-L-11C turboshafts.
Dimensions: Tandem main (three-blade) rotor diameter 60ft (18·29m); fuselage length 51ft (15·54m); height 18ft 7in (5·67m).
Weights: Empty 20,616lb (9351kg); maximum loaded 46,000lb (20,865kg).
Performance: Maximum speed 180mph (290km/h) at 10,200ft (3110m); average cruising speed 160mph (257km/h); mission radius 115 miles (185km).
Armament: One 7·62mm door-mounted machine gun.
Accommodation: Two pilots, one crew chief or combat commander, 33 to 44 troops, or 24 litters with two attendants, or vehicles and freight. Up to 28,000lb (12,700kg) can be carried on external cargo hook.
History: First flight 14 October 1967; delivery of production models began in spring of 1968; first deployed to Vietnam in September 1968.
User: US Army.

continued ▶

Right: Typical of front-line resupply missions, bringing a water-trailer to the 12th Infantry, in the Central Highlands.

Below: This CH-47A was pictured in support of South Korean troops in Cambodia in summer 1970. Note blue dolphin insignia on tail.

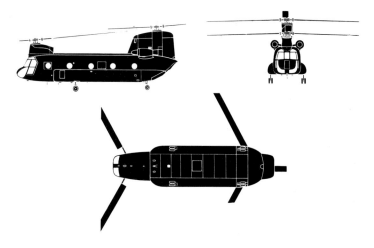

Above: Three-view of CH-47 (all models similar).

►Tactical employment: In December 1962 the CH-47A was delivered for US Army testing and pilot training. It participated in the Army's evaluation of the air mobility concept and became operational with the First Cavalry Division (Air Mobile), formerly the 11th Air Assault Division. In October 1963 it was classified as the US Army's standard medium transport helicopter.

The Chinook arrived in South Vietnam in 1965 and served with the First Cavalry and the 147th Helicopter Company. It proved an invaluable aircraft for artillery movement and heavy logistics, but was seldom used as an assault troop transport. The CH-47 was particularly useful in placing artillery batteries atop mountain positions that were inaccessible by any other means and then keeping them resupplied with ammunition. Operational experience disclosed that the Chinooks were limited to 7,000 pounds (3171kg) payload when operating in mountainous areas. The early designs were also limited by the rotor system which did not permit full use of the installed power.

During Operation Pershing in the spring of 1967 the Chinook was adapted for bombing missions. It dropped 29,600 pounds (13,408kg) of tear gas on enemy underground fortifications and tunnels in Binh Dinh province. The tear gas drums were rolled out of the craft's back door and its fuzing system armed by a static line once the drums were clear of the helicopter. Also fitted with napalm drums, a single Chinook could drop 5,000 pounds (2265kg) on targets which could not be reached by fixed wing aircraft.

The First Cavalry tested three of the helicopters as gunships. Armed with two 20mm Gatling guns, 40mm grenade launchers, and ·50 caliber machine guns, the Chinooks were nicknamed Go-Go Birds and proved extremely popular with the troops they supported. However, two of the helicopters were lost and the experiment of the large armed aircraft was given up.

During the battle for Hue in February 1968 the CH-47 flew between the battlefield and cargo ships offshore in what was claimed to be the first ship-to-shore resupply in combat.

In June 1970 Chinooks of the 228th Helicopter Battalion swooped in low along the valleys and in bad weather to rescue beleaguered forces of the 1st Battalion, 50th Cavalry in their withdrawal from Cambodia. Operating under heavy fire, one helicopter was shot down and five others damaged.

In June 1970 Chonooks of the 228th Helicopter Battalion swooped in On one occasion, 147 refugees and their possessions were evacuated on a single flight. Chonooks were credited with the recovery of 11,500 disabled aircraft worth more than $3 billion.

Below: Boeing Vertol CH-47 Chinook (22137) US Army, Vietnam.

Above: Start of Operation Pegasus to relieve Khe Sanh, 1 April 1968; the CH-47A has brought troops of the 1st Cavalry Division.

22137

TATES ARMY

Cessna A-37 Dragonfly

A-37A, B.

Origin: Cessna Aircraft Company.
Type: Two-seat, light strike aircraft.
Engines: Two 2,850lb (1293kg) thrust General Electric J85-17A single-shaft turbojets.
Dimensions: Span over tip tanks 35ft 10½in (10·93m); length overall 29ft 3½in (8·93m); height overall 8ft 10½in (2·70m).
Weight: Empty, equipped 5,843lb (2650kg); maximum takeoff and landing 14,000lb (4858kg).
Performance: Maximum level speed at 16,000ft (4875m) 507mph (816km/h); maximum cruising speed at 25,000ft (7620m), 489mph (787km/h); range (maximum weapons) 460 miles (740km); range (maximum fuel) 1,012 miles (1678km).
Armament: One GAU-2B/A.7·62mm minigun installed in forward fuselage. Each wing, four pylons: two inner ones can carry 800lb (363kg) each, intermediate one 600lb (272kg) and outer one 500lb (227kg); maximum ordnance load 5,680lb (2576kg).
History: First flight (XT-37) 12 October 1954; (YAT-37D) 22 October 1963; (A-37B) September 1967.
Users: US Air Force, South Vietnamese Air Force.

Tactical employment: Once the A-37A had successfully undergone testing, the US Air Force adapted the A-37B, the production version which was fitted for aerial refueling. As part of the modernization plan for the South Vietnamese Air Force, the USAF sought to convert three VNAF A-1 fighter squadrons to A-37 jets. On 1 January 1968 the first squadron to receive A-37s stood down in preparation for conversion, and the following month the first 18 VNAF pilots departed for the United States to begin transition training. Actual squadron conversion began with delivery of the first A-37 jets from the US so that by May 1969 the full complement of 54 A-37B jets were on hand and assigned to the 524th, 520th, and 516th Fighter Squadrons. Other Dragonfly units quickly took shape, and the light easily maintained A-37 became South Vietnam's principal strike aircraft.

The A-37 was one of the last Vietnam-based strike aircraft used by the 7th Air Force. During the siege of An Loc, in the 1972 North Vietnamese Easter Offensive, the Dragonfly flew strike missions in the hands of American and South Vietnamese crews. The A-37 remained a part of the South Vietnamese Air Force inventory until the fall of Saigon.

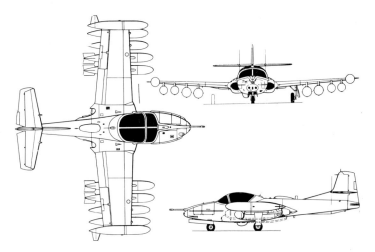

Above: A-37B Dragonfly with maximum external load.

Above: An A-37B of USAF 8th Tac Ftr Wing on return from a bombing mission over North Vietnam in September 1972. At a distance the Dragonflies of the VNAF looked almost identical.

Left: A fully armed A-37B of the VNAF, parked with O-1E Bird Dog FAC platforms.

Cessna O-1 Bird Dog

O-1E, F, G (originally US Army L-19).

Origin: Cessna Aircraft Company.

Type: Two-place observation plane.

Engine: One 213hp Continental 0-470-11 air cooled type.

Dimensions: Span 36ft (10·9m); length 25ft 10in (7·89m); height 7ft 1in (2·23m).

Weight: Empty 1,614lb (680kg); loaded 2,400–2,430lb (1090–1103kg), (F) 2,800lb (1272·7kg).

Performance: Maximum speed 115mph (184km/h); cruising speed at 5,000ft (1525m) 104mph (166·4km/h); cruising range 530 miles (848km).

Armament: Target marking rockets.

History: First contract placed by US Army June 1950; by October 1954 Cessna had delivered 2,426 L-19As to the Army and sixteen OE-1s to the Marine Corps; production resumed 1957–1958 and again in 1961, until a grand total of 3,431 had been built.

Users: US Air Force Tactical Air Command, US Marine Corps, US Army, South Vietnamese Air Force, Royal Lao Air Force.

Tactical employment: As late as 1968, the Bird Dog served a majority of the forward air controllers in Southeast Asia. Either flying alone or carrying a second crewman, these pilots searched out targets, marked them, determined the location of friendly troops, and directed air strikes. In the early years of the conflict, the O-1 patrolled the roads over which friendly truck convoys passed, searching for ambush sites. For a time, the mere presence of one of these planes served as a deterrent, since the enemy was reluctant to open fire, reveal his location, and invite attack by fighters controlled by the slowly circling Bird Dog. The Viet Cong and North Vietnamese soon grew bolder, however, and any group that believed it had been sighted would open fire, trying to bring down the forward air controller and reduce the accuracy of the impending strike.

The presence overhead of a Bird Dog could mean survival for embattled American or South Vietnamese units. Smoke from carefully placed rockets brought swift destruction upon the enemy and also prevented accidental bombing of friendly troops. On occasion, infantry officers had to call for strikes so close to their men that some were certain to be killed or wounded; they had to make the cruel but crucial decision that to risk some casualties would ensure the survival of their command.

Forward air controllers found targets that the crew of a fast-moving jet could never have seen. Foot prints on a mud flat, for instance, revealed to one controller the direction that a Viet Cong battalion had followed. He located the force near a bluff and called in devastating air strikes.

Although it performed valuable service, the O-1 had serious short-comings. It lacked armor or self-sealing fuel tanks, its range was short, and it carried too few rockets. Yet, when a suitable replacement arrived, the planes passed into the hands of South Vietnamese or Lao airmen.

Right: Cessna O-1 Bird Dogs were far from new during the Vietnam War though a few were built after 1960. Here the most common variant, an O-1E, is seen from another during FAC operations.

Below: another O-1E—aircraft O-12889—on a low-level FAC mission operating from Pleiku AB in the Central Highlands.

Cessna O-2

O-2A, B.

Origin: Cessna Aircraft Company.
Type: Two-place observation plane.
Engines: Two 210hp Continental IO-360-C air-cooled piston engines in tractor-pusher arrangement.
Dimensions: Span 38ft (11·58m); length 29ft 9in (9·07m); height 9ft 4in (2·84m).
Weight: Empty 2,848lb (1294·5kg); loaded 5,400lb (2454·5kg).
Performance: Maximum speed 199mph (320km/h) at sea level; cruising speed 144mph (232km/h) at 1,000ft (305m); range 1,060 miles (1706km).
Armament: (A) normally marking rockets only, though each of the four underwing hard points could accommodate a 7·62mm minigun pack.
History: Adapted from a business aircraft first flown 28 February 1961; ordered by the US Air Force 29 December 1966.
User: US Air Force Tactical Air Command, PACAF.

Tactical employment: The O-2A, with greater range and double the number of target marking rockets, served as stopgap replacement for the O-1 until the North American OV-10A arrived on the scene. At least one of the Bird Dog's shortcomings had not been corrected, however, for the newer Cessna also lacked adequate armor.

Below: Though the O-1 series remained active in Vietnam, the O-2 was demonstrably superior. This O-2B was pictured in 1967 over Nha Trang, which also suffered in WW2 and 1950–53.

Above: The regular O-2A, of which 346 were delivered to the USAF, had four wing pylons for a variety of stores.

The O-2B flew psychological warfare missions, using a high-powered broadcasting set with three 600-watt amplifiers and a hand-operated leaflet dispenser. These planes urged the Viet Cong and North Vietnamese to surrender and offered messages of encouragement to those loyal to the Saigon government. Propaganda, however, formed just a part of their work, for the rules of engagement required that villagers living in territory under South Vietnamese control had to receive warning of impending air or ground attack by American or government forces. Loudspeaker broadcasts normally preceded counterthrusts against North Vietnamese or Viet Cong who had seized populated areas.

de Havilland C-7

C-7A (formerly AC-1B and CV-2B), Caribou.

Origin: The de Havilland Aircraft Co. of Canada.
Type: STOL transport.
Engines: Two 1,450hp Pratt & Whitney R-2000-7M2 radials.
Dimensions: Span 95ft 7½in (29·15m); length 72ft 7in (22·13m); height 31ft 9in (9·7m).
Weight: Operating weight 18,260lb (8283kg); maximum payload 8,740lb (3965kg); normal maximum takeoff weight 28,500lb (12,928kg).
Performance: Maximum speed 216mph (347km/h) at 6,500ft (1980m); economical cruising speed 182mph (293km/h) at 7,500ft (2285m); maximum range 1,307 miles (2013km).
Armament: None.
Flight crew: Three.
History: First flight 30 July 1958; the first of five evaluation models delivered to the US Army on 8 October 1959; deliveries of production aircraft began in January 1961.
Users: US Army (AC-1, CV-2B); US Air Force (C-7A); Royal Australian Air Force (Caribou).

Tactical employment: The de Havilland company designed the Caribou to operate from short, hurriedly built airstrips, a characteristic that appealed to the US Army. As a result, the Army ordered five of the planes, evaluated them, and made this type its standard transport. These AC-1s, soon re-designated CV-2Bs, fitted well into the Army's evolving theory of air mobility, for they could carry troops and cargo to forward airfields where helicopters would take over, distributing the men and supplies among front-line units.

Once the Army became involved in the Vietnam fighting, however, the CV-2B required help from Air Force tactical transports. When airmobile troops attacked the enemy in the Ia Drang Valley during the fall of 1965, the Caribous rushed fuel and cargo to forward bases for further distribution by truck and helicopter. The demands of the rapidly moving assault force exceeded the capacity of the available Army transports, and Air Force C-123s and C-130s had to join in the operation. The CV-2B proved most effective in delivering supplies, sometimes by parachute, to the Special Forces camps established along South Vietnam's western border.

Below: A Caribou of the RAAF taking aboard passengers and cargo at Vung Tau AB (Cap St Jacques) in 1966.

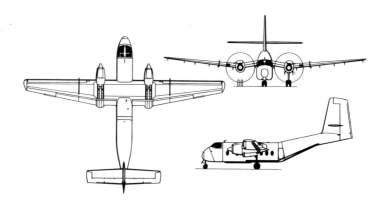

Above: Three-view of C-7 (maker's designation, DHC-4).

Responsible for tactical airlift, the US Air Force sought to take over the Army Caribous and operate them in conjunction with the C-130s and C-123s. The Air Force and Army chiefs of staff, Generals John P. McConnell and Harold K. Johnson, negotiated an agreement under which the Air Force took over these transports on 1 January 1967. The Army retained the right to develop and operate large helicopters and kept its Grumman OV-1 battlefield reconnaissance planes.

Under Air Force control, the C-7A, as the plane now was known, continued to support the Special Forces camps and other remote outposts even though it was part of a centralized airlift system. The Caribou remained the logical choice for such work because of its handling characteristics. This transport could clear a fifty foot (15 meter) barrier after a takeoff run of 1,185 feet (361 meters) or land over the same obstacle within a distance of 1,235 feet (376 meters).

Before the Caribou came under Air Force control, one of the planes had served as an airborne command post for the 1st Cavalry Division (Airmobile). An array of radio equipment enabled the division commander to remain in contact with subordinate units and higher headquarters.

Nor were the American armed services alone in using the Caribou in Southeast Asia. A few Australian aircraft of this type served in South Vietnam. Although incorporated into the centralized airlift network, the primary mission of these Caribou transports was support of an Australian task force. Finally, thanks to Vietnamization, the South Vietnamese Air Force eventually received some 50 C-7As.

Douglas A-1 Skyraider

A-1E, H, J.

Origin: Douglas Aircraft Company, California.
Type: Two-place (E) or single-seat (H, J) single-engine land or carrier-based multipurpose attack bomber or utility aircraft.
Engine: (E) one R-3350-26WA/WD 2,700hp; (H) one R-3350-26WC/WC; (J) one R-3350-26WB.
Dimensions: Span 50ft 9in (15·49m); length 38ft 10in (11·84m).
Weight: (H, J) empty 10,550lb (4795kg); gross 25,000lb (11,340kg).
Performance: (H, J) maximum speed 318mph (512km/h); cruising speed 188mph (313km/h); range, to 3,000 miles (4830km) with external tanks.
Armament: (H, J) four fixed forward-firing 20mm cannon. Up to 8,000lb (3600kg) external ordnance. ***continued▶***

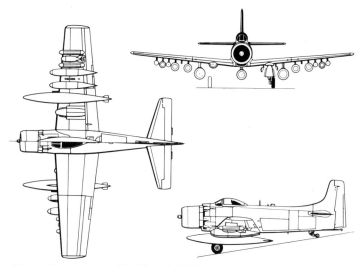

Above: Three-view of A-1H or A-1J single-seat model.

Left: Using an MJ-1 bomb loader to put a canister of Igloo White Spikebuoy sensors aboard an A-1E at Nakhon Phanom AB, 1968.

Below: A-1H single-seat Skyraiders of the VNAF; thought obsolete in 1950, by 1970 this capable machine was better appreciated.

Right: with its pylons empty a two-seat A-1E rolls down into light cloud to begin strafing passes on a surface target during the Vietnam war. Very effective, though rather more vulnerable than jet attack aircraft, the A-1 scored in weapon load and flight endurance, the latter being extended to a theoretical 12 hours with maximum fuel.

▶**History:** In September 1962 all Skyraiders in service were redesignated in the A-1 series.

Users: US Air Force, US Navy, and South Vietnam Air Force.

Tactical employment: Besides serving the US Navy the A-1E was adopted by the US Air Force's Tactical Air Command. This command acquired 50 Navy A-1s to equip the first Air Commando Group engaged in Counterinsurgency (Coin) operations supporting the South Vietnamese forces. The US Navy used several types of the A-1 in Vietnam, including electronic counter-measure versions.

In 1967 the Navy pulled its remaining A-1s out of Vietnam leaving the US Air Force and the South Vietnamese Air Force as the prime users of the commonly called "Spad". At the time of the January 1973 truce, about 100 A-1s were turned over to the South Vietnamese and several squadrons were still operational at the time of the fall of South Vietnam in 1975. The US Air Force had disbanded the last of its Spad units in the fall of 1974.

The A-1 had a varied role in Vietnam, such as flying rescue, close air support and forward air control (FAC) missions. The aircraft was credited with many achievements in its combat role in Southeast Asia. For example, in December 1964, VNAF A-1Hs and USAF A-1Es inflicted more than 400 casualties and were credited with averting the destruction of a regional force company near Long My after that unit's resupply convoy had been ambushed.

In August 1965 Air Force A-1Es began escorting rescue units. During a typical recovery operation, two A-1Es flew directly to the general search area and looked for some sign of the downed crewmen while two other A-1Es escorted the helicopter to the area. If it was determined that the pilot was in a hostile area, the A-1Es would commence attacking with bombs, rockets and 20mm cannon fire suppressing the defenses so the helicopter could land.

In March 1966 A-1Es of the First Air Commando Squadron braved bad weather to go to the aid of a Special Forces Camp in the A Shau Valley which was under attack by a force of 2,000 North Vietnamese regulars. In the midst of the battle the A-1E pilots found a hole in the thick overcast that blanketed the mountainous area and flew 210 strikes that slowed the enemy advance. The A-1Es received credit for killing some 500 of the enemy. General Westmoreland later called the air support on this occasion one of the most courageous displays of airmanship in aviation history.

During that same encounter a Major Bernard F. Fisher, an A-1 pilot of the First Air Commando Squadron, saw one of his fellow airmen make an emergency landing on the A Shau airstrip as the North Vietnamese were overrunning the camp. Major Fisher landed his aircraft, maneuvered it in broken-field fashion down the debris-littered runway, braked to a halt, turned, picked-up his comrade, and took off through enemy fire. For this incredible rescue Major Fisher received the Medal of Honor.

But perhaps one of the most memorable feats of the Spad while in Vietnam took place on 20 June 1965. Four Spads from the carrier USS *Midway* were on a rescue combat air patrol (ResCap) mission when suddenly they were attacked by two MiG-17s. The Skyraiders dived for the ground and made a defensive "scissored" maneuver just above the tree tops. In a dog fight lasting five minutes the four prop pilots kept turning inside the faster jets until two of the Navy airmen got behind one of the MiGs and shot it down. The surviving North Vietnamese fighter fled. The maneuverability that proved so effective in supporting ground troops had paid off in aerial combat.

Below: A dramatic photograph of an attack on a surface target with a phosphorus bomb, a thermal weapon used as an alternative to napalm on targets of uncertain position. The aircraft was an A-1E, pulling out with vortices from the wingtips.

Douglas A-26 Invader

A-26A, B, C, B-26B, B-26C, B-26K, RB-26C.

Origin: Douglas Aircraft.

Type: Twin-engine attack bomber and reconnaissance plane.

Engine: Two 2,000hp Pratt and Whitney R-2800-71 air-cooled radials with two-speed superchargers.

Dimensions: Span 70ft (21·35m), length 50ft 9in (15·47m); height 18ft 6in (5·64m).

Weight: Normal loaded weight 27,000lb (12,260kg); maximum permissible loaded weight 32,000lb (14,530kg).

Performance: Maximum speed (normal rated power) 359mph (574·4km/h) at 16,700ft (5090m); cruising speed (2/3 power) 266mph (425km/h) at 5,000ft (1525m); service ceiling 28,500ft (8690m).

Armament: Standard armament of A-26B consisted of 18 ·50 caliber (12·7mm) machine guns, six in nose (four on starboard side and two on port side), four under each wing outboard of propeller discs in twin package mountings; the bomb bay could accommodate a maximum of four 1,000lb (454kg) bombs. A maximum of four 500lb (227kg) bombs could be carried under the wings when the bomb-bay load was reduced to six 500lb bombs.

History: XA-26 flown for first time 10 July 1942.

Users: French Air Force, US Air Force.

Tactical employment: A veteran of World War II, the A-26 was redesignated B-26 after that conflict and then given its original classification as an attack plane. According to legend, the US State Department at one time did not want to acknowledge the use of bombers in Southeast Asia and insisted that the B-26 become the A-26. In fact, the change probably stemmed from the mission the plane was performing, night interdiction, which more closely resembled attack aviation than light bombardment.

To add to the confusion over nomenclature, the Air Force adopted the YB-26K Counterinvader, a B-26B redesigned for counterinsurgency warfare by On Mark Engineering. Some 50 planes were modified to B-26K standard, fitted with fourteen forward-firing ·50 caliber machine guns, given additional fuel tanks and bomb pylons, then rechristened A-26As.

Nor was this Douglas aircraft a stranger to this part of the world. Already during the Indochina War, French B-26Bs and Cs, with guns in the nose for strafing, or a plexiglas bombardier's compartment, had carried the war to the Viet Minh, attacking communist troop concentrations and gun positions or flying armed reconnaissance against columns of coolies delivering supplies.

Below: This Invader, an ex-WW2 A-26B, was serving with the French Armée de l'Air in Indo-China in the early 1950s.

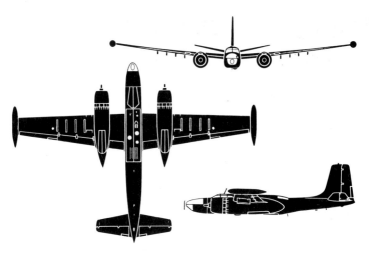

Above: Three-view of remanufactured B-26K, later restyled A-26A.

Above: A fine night shot of an On Mark A-26A (ex-B26K) of the
609th Special Missions Sqn at Nakhon Phanom RTAFB, July 1969.

The camera-equipped RB-26C conducted aerial reconnaissance for the
French Air Force.

The same B-26 or A-26 variants saw action with the US Air Force
during the early years of American involvement in the Vietnam conflict.
Metal fatigue in the wing structure caused the grounding of these planes
late in 1964. The reconnaissance version, outperformed by newer aircraft
like the RF-101 Voodoo or OV-1 Mohawk, disappeared from the scene, but
the bomber, refurbished and reclassified an attack plane, returned to combat.

Recognizing the need for an aircraft that could remain on station for a
long time, patiently searching out and attacking an enemy concealed by
jungle, night, or bad weather, the Air Force deployed eight A-26s, fitted out
for night operations, to Nakhon Phanom, Thailand, in June 1966. These
aircraft flew hunter-killer missions against truck convoys in southern Laos.
The A-26s replaced the slow, vulnerable AC-47 gunship until they were
themselves succeeded by sensor-equipped AC-119K or AC-130.

Douglas C-47

C-47D, VC-47D, EC-47D, AC-47D, RC-47D.

Origin: Douglas Aircraft.
Type: Transport (C-47D, VC-47D); electronic reconnaissance craft (EC-47D); gunship (AC-47D); reconnaissance plane (RC-47D).
Engines: Two 1,200hp Pratt & Whitney R-1830-92 radials.
Dimensions: Span 95ft (28·9m); length 64ft 5½in (19·63m); height 16ft 11½in (5·2m).
Weights: Empty, about 16,970lb (7700kg); loaded, about 25,200lb (11,423kg); overload limit 33,000lb (14,969kg).
Performance: (C-47D) maximum speed 229mph (368km/h) at 8,500ft (2590m); cruising speed 185mph (296km/h); normal range 1,500 miles (2400km)
Armament: (AC-47D) three 7·62-mm multibarrel machine guns.
Flight crew: Two (C-47D) to seven (AC-47D).
History: Derived from the Douglas DC-3, which first flew on 17 December 1935; those C-47s retained after World War II were standardized according to mission and redesignated as D models.
Users: US Air Force Tactical Air Command, PACAF (AC-47D, EC-47D, C-47D); French Air Force, Royal Laotian Air Force (AC-47D, C-47D); South Vietnamese Air Force.

Tactical employment: French forces serving in Indochina had some 70 of these planes, though there rarely were crews enough to fly that many at the same time. The famous World War II transport, which the French called the Dakota, was the backbone of the tactical airlift fleet. These planes parachuted the expeditionary forces into Dien Bien Phu and then struggled unsuccessfully to sustain these men in their battle against a relentless foe. Although the C-47D served from the outset of America's Southeast Asia involvement, flying courier and occasional reconnaissance missions, the transport version, nicknamed "Gooney Bird", never achieved the prominence it had earned during World War II and the Korean conflict. Newer transports outperformed the elderly aircraft. Even the de Havilland C-7A, the smallest

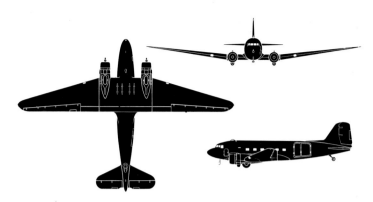

Above: Three-view of C-47 with freight door and air-drop racks.

of this new breed of cargo hauler, carried as large a payload as the C-47D and was loaded more easily through a door at the rear of the cargo compartment. The old transport, however, performed especially useful service in the hands of Lao and South Vietnamese airmen, who found it durable, easily maintained, and comparatively simple to fly. A more luxurious model, the VC-47D, served as an executive transport for high-ranking officers.

Whatever its limitations as a transport, variants of the C-47D functioned successfully in other roles. The electronic reconnaissance version, the EC-47D, patrolled South Vietnam's western border and the coastal waters off southern North Vietnam, picking up enemy radio signals. Operators on board these planes obtained bearings to the transmitter and, by means of triangulation, intelligence specialists determined the location of the headquarters where the broadcasts originated. The EC-47Ds, together with the US Army's modified Beechcraft U-21s that flew the same mission through- ▶

Below: C-47s—probably C-47Bs of an Air Commando Squadron— in standard USAF camouflage for transports in Vietnam. The prefix O to the serial number denotes over ten years old.

▶ out much of South Vietnam, provided valuable information for the planning of strikes by tactical fighters or B-52s.

The South Vietnamese used their few RC-47s for visual rather than photographic reconnaissance. On a typical mission, an observer peered through the glass of the camera bay in search of coastal junks smuggling ammunition or supplies from North Vietnam.

The venerable transport, often older than some of the crew members who flew it, also provided the air frame for an important tactical innovation, the gunship. Experience in South Vietnam soon demonstrated that fast-moving jet fighters, summoned to the aid of an outpost under night attack by the Viet Cong, had difficulty pinpointing targets before running low on fuel. In these circumstances, speed and maneuverability were not essential, for the enemy depended upon darkness and jungle growth, rather than anti-aircraft weapons, for defense against air attack. What was needed was an airplane that could patrol throughout the night, locate the enemy, and direct a torrent of accurate fire upon him.

Among those who tackled the problem of nighttime defense of outposts was Captain Ronald Terry of the US Air Force Aeronautical Systems Division. He remembered reading about flying missionaries in Latin America who lowered baskets of supplies on a rope from a tightly circling airplane. Throughout the series of pylon turns, the basket remained suspended over a selected point on the ground. Could this principle be applied to fire from automatic weapons? Terry believed it could, and tests proved him right.

The captain's experiments prepared the way for Puff the Magic Dragon, a C-47D gunship prototype that entered service in 1965. Crews at first called their plane the FC-47, a designation that seemed to annoy fighter pilots and, for whatever the reason, soon gave way to AC-47. Puff's "flare kicker" illuminated the target; the pilot then used a mark on the window to his left as a gun sight and circled slowly as three multibarrel 7·62mm machine guns fired 18,000 rounds per minute from the door and two windows in the port side of the passenger compartment.

Below: One of the first photographs to be taken of Puff the Magic Dragon, an AC-47 with three 7·62mm Miniguns installed in the left side for hand-aimed firing at ground targets, usually while circling by night. The photograph was released in March 1966.

Above: One of several major new installations in C-47s for the Vietnam war was the psy-war loudspeaker; 5th Air Commando Sqn.

Puff the Magic Dragon, flame billowing from its guns, proved so successful that the Air Force created two squadrons of AC-47Ds. The standard version, called Spooky, carried the same armament and equipment as the prototype, and the seven-man crew operated in the same way. Although unable to survive against the anti-aircraft defenses in southern Laos, these first gunships performed ably in helping defend outposts within South Vietnam. The US Air Force was sufficiently impressed to develop improved gunships, fitted with radar, infrared sensors, and light intensification devices for finding an enemy concealed by darkness. Faster, more heavily armed, and able to fly higher than the AC-47D, these new models would be able to attack truck traffic over supply lines defended by anti-aircraft concentrations. Out of this program emerged Gunship II, using the Lockheed C-130, and Gunship III, derived from the Fairchild C-119.

Above: Despite careful security US air bases were frequently attacked by the Viet Cong. Here C-47s are seen at dispersal.

Douglas C-133 Cargomaster

C-133A, B.

Origin: Douglas Aircraft.
Type: Transport.
Engines: (A) four 6,500hp Pratt & Whitney T34-P-7WA turboprops, (B) four 7,500hp Pratt & Whitney T34-P-9WA turboprops.
Dimensions: Span 179ft 8in (54·75m); length 157ft 6½in (48·0m); height 48ft 3in (14·7m).
Weight: (B) empty 120,363lb (54,595kg); normal takeoff weight 286,000lb (129,730kg).
Performance: (B) maximum speed at 9,000ft (27·40m) 347mph (558km/h); normal cruising speed 310mph (500km/h); range with payload of 43,706lb (19,825kg) and maximum fuel 4,360 miles (7015km).
Armament: None.
Flight crew: Five.
History: First production model completed February 1956 and flown 23 April 1956; production ended April 1961.
User: US Air Force Military Airlift Command.

Tactical employment: During the build-up of American ground forces in 1965, the Military Airlift Command became hard-pressed for cargo aircraft. The C-141A was just entering service, the C-135 was better suited to carrying passengers than war materiel, and the C-130Es assigned to the command remained basically tactical, rather than long-range, transports. The Douglas C-124A boasted a cavernous cargo hold, but the lumbering aircraft required some 95 hours' flying time for a round trip between Travis Air Force Base, California, and Tan Son Nhut airfield at Saigon. Almost by default, the three squadrons of C-133As and Bs emerged as the best of the trans-Pacific cargo carriers, even though they suffered recurring and sometimes fatal problems with their turboprop engines.

The C-133 featured a cargo compartment accessible by means of a ramp and clamshell doors at the rear. Military vehicles as large as bulldozers could negotiate the ramp and enter a hold that measured 90 feet (27·4 meters) in length and was wide enough to accommodate a pair of strategic ballistic missiles stowed side by side. Other typical loads might consist of

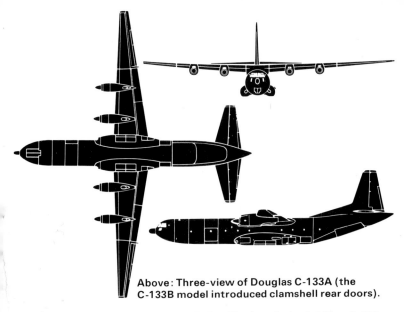

Above: Three-view of Douglas C-133A (the C-133B model introduced clamshell rear doors).

20 jet engines or 16 loaded jeeps. Rollers like those in the C-123 or C-130, could be installed in the floor of the storage area to facilitate the handling of cargo pallets.

Throughout the Southeast Asia conflict, the USAF Military Airlift Command faced shortages of crews and aircraft like those that had arisen during the 1965 deployments. Members of the Air Force Reserve flew as crew members on transport missions to Southeast Asia even though their units were not called to active duty. Reservists also formed complete crews for the new C-141As, supplementing the work of the regular crews in order to ensure maximum use of these aircraft.

Below: In its day the C-133 was a giant, much larger (and longer-ranged) than the C-130 seen on the right. It did a big and unsung job in the SE Asia war, but thereafter was withdrawn.

Douglas C-124 Globemaster II

C-124A, C.

Origin: Douglas Aircraft.
Type: Transport.
Engines: (A) four 3,500hp Pratt & Whitney R-4360-2W radials; (C) four 3,800hp Pratt & Whitney R-4360-63 piston radials.
Dimensions: Span 174ft 1½in (53·10m); length 130ft 5in (39·77m); height 48ft 3½in (14·72m).
Weight: Loaded 175,000lb (79,450kg).
Performance: (A) normal cruising speed 230mph (370km/h); range 4,050 miles (6485km) with 50,000lb (22,680kg) payload, 1,300 miles (1930km) with 100,000lb (45,360kg) payload.
Armament: None.
Flight crew: Five.
History: First flight of prototype, 27 November 1949; production ended 9 May 1955 after the delivery of 445 aircraft.
User: US Air Force Military Airlift Command.

Tactical employment: When it entered service, the Globemaster II could accommodate all types of Army weapons and vehicles, except for the largest tanks, artillery pieces, and trucks. The cargo hold provided 10,000 cubic feet (283 cubic meters) of usable space and could be entered by means of an elevator in the belly of the plane or over a ramp that extended through clamshell doors in the nose below the added radar. Two overhead cranes installed within the stowage compartment facilitated cargo handling. A second deck could be installed in the plane's interior, enabling the C-124

Douglas RB-66 and EA-3B

RB-66B, C, EB-66B, C, E, A-3B, KA-3B, EA-3B,

Origin: Douglas Aircraft.
Type: Three-place light bomber (A-3B); reconnaissance plane (RB-66B); electronic warfare craft (some RB-66Bs, RB-66C—redesignated EB-66B, C—EB-66E, EA-3B); aerial tanker (KA-3B, EKA-3B).
Engines: (Air Force models) two 10,200lb (4626kg) thrust Allison J71-A-13 turbojets, (Navy models) two 12,400lb (5624kg) thrust Pratt & Whitney J57-P-10 turbojets.
Dimensions: Span 72ft 6in (22·10m); length 76ft 4in (23·27m); height 22ft 9in (6·94m), (Air Force models) 23ft 7in (7·18m).
Weight: (A-3B) normal takeoff weight 73,000lb (33,112kg).
Performance: (A-3B) maximum speed 610mph (982km/h) at 10,000ft (3050m); operating radius 1,050 miles (1690km).
Armament: (A-3B) two radar-aimed 20mm cannon in tail turret.
History: RB-66B first flight 28 June 1954; deliveries began 1 February 1956; RB-66C first flight 29 October 1955; deliveries began 11 May 1956; EA-3B (rebuild) first flight 10 December 1958.
Users: US Air Force Tactical Air Command, PACAF (RB-66B, C, EB-66B, C, E); US Navy (A-3B, EA-3B, KA-3B, EKA-3B).

Tactical employment: The B-66 Destroyer and A-3 Skywarrior shared a common ancestor, the XA3D-1, first flown in October 1952. Fitted with more powerful engines, this prototype evolved into the A3D-2, redesignated the A-3B. Because of its speed, which was comparable to fighters of that era, the Skywarrior's only armament was a pair of 20mm cannon in a remotely controlled tail turret. By 1971, the A-3B had undergone conversion to

Above: A C-124 in service with MATS (Military Air Transport Ser-Service, later MAC); A and C versions ultimately looked similar.

to carry 200 troops or 179 wounded, 127 stretcher patients and the rest seated.

By the time of the 1965 Vietnam build-up, the C-124 had seen its best days. Its metal skin had wrinkled, its engines required frequent maintenance, and it could seldom attain its rated speed. Yet, the Air Force had more Globemaster IIs than any other cargo aircraft. These planes and other C-124s belonging to the Air Force Reserve helped establish transpacific service until the C-141A became available.

Above: An EKA-3B Skywarrior of the Navy arrives at Da Nang AB in April 1966. This was a versatile and capable aircraft.

electronic warfare duties or had become aerial tankers.

The Air Force also purchased a bomber based on the XA3D-1, calling it▶

▶the B-66B. Although the B-66B saw no combat in Southeast Asia, a reconnaissance version did. Besides photographing portions of South Vietnam, this model used its navigational gear to serve as pathfinder for fighter-bombers attacking targets in North Vietnam during the early weeks of Operation Rolling Thunder.

The RB-66 also carried out electronic warfare missions. The RB-66C (later redesignated EB-66C) featured a pressurized capsule, installed in the bomb bay, that accommodated four technicians who operated electronic reconnaissance gear. Some RB-66Bs carried jamming transmitters for disrupting enemy radar. These models—later redesignated EB-66Bs and, after minor modification, EB-66Es—lacked the speed to accompany fighter-bombers over the target and had to perform their jamming from a distance.

Until the arrival of these Air Force electronic warfare planes, Marine Corps EF-10Bs and Navy EA-1Fs did most of the radar jamming, even though they lacked the transmitting power of the larger plane. The Navy EA-3B performed the same missions—electronic reconnaissance and some jamming—as the EB-66C, which it closely resembled.

Skywarriors also served as flying tankers for carrier-based strike forces. Removal of the electronic warfare capsule from the bomb bay of the EA-3B, substitution of a fuel tank, and addition of pumps and hoses for probe-and-drogue refueling converted the plane into an EKA-3B. When the A-3B grew too old to serve as a light bomber, it also joined the tanker force, becoming the KA-3B.

Right: A remarkable vertical photograph showing a flight of Thuds —F-105Ds— dropping 3,000lb bombs triggered by RB-66C lead.

Above: EB-66Es (converted RB-66Bs) parked at Takhli RTAFB on Christmas Day 1968. Electronics cost more than original aircraft.

Below: An EB-66E on takeoff; almost five short tons of electronics were carried, with numerous antennae.

Fairchild C-119

C-119G; AC-119G Shadow, AC-119K Stinger.

Origin: Fairchild Hiller Corporation.
Type: Transport, gunship.
Engines: (G models) two Wright R-3350-89B 3,700hp radial engines; (K) the two Wright radials and two auxiliary General Electric J85-GE 17 turbojets, each developing 2,850lb (1293kg) thrust, mounted in under-wing pods.
Dimensions: Span 109ft 3in (33·32m); length 86ft 6in (26·38m); height 26ft 3in (8·0m).
Weight: (C-119G) empty 39,982lb (18,152kg); payload 28,000lb (12,712kg); maximum takeoff weight 74,400lb (33,778kg); (AC-119K) empty 58,282lb (26,436kg); basic operating weight 60,995lb (27,649kg); maximum takeoff weight 80,400lb (36,468kg).
Performance: (C-119G) cruising speed 200mph (320km/h); range 2,280 miles (3648km); (AC-119K) maximum cruising speed at 10.000ft (3050m) without using jet engines 173mph (278km/h), using jet engines 219mph (352km/h); range with maximum load 1,980 miles (3186km).
Armament: (AC-119G) four 7·62mm multibarrel machine guns; (AC-119K) four 7·62mm miniguns and two 20mm multibarrel cannon.
Flight crew: (C-119G) four; (gunships) eight to ten.
History: The C-119A prototype, a modified Fairchild C-82, first flew in November 1947; the YC-119K with auxiliary jet engines first flew in February 1967.
Users: US Air Force Tactical Air Command, PACAF (AC-119G, K); South Vietnamese Air Force.

Tactical employment: The South Vietnamese Air Force received the C-119G to satisfy the need for a transport able to carry cargo too bulky for the C-47D. Unlike the narrow-bodied Douglas transport, which had to be loaded through a troop door in the port side, the Flying Boxcar featured clam shell doors at the rear of the cargo compartment that opened wide enough to admit light trucks or artillery pieces. Because of its age and the resulting scarcity of spare parts, C-119G maintenance proved a problem.

Despite this difficulty, the US Air Force cast the G model in the role of gunship, fitting it out with four 7.62mm multibarrel machine guns, aimed obliquely downward from the port side, and adding a computerized fire control system that helped the pilot keep the weapons trained on target. To locate these targets, the eight-man crew of the AC-119G Shadow used flares, a searchlight, and a night observation device that intensified natural light. During 1969, a US Air Force special operations squadron began flying nighttime combat missions in the Shadow, and the type later passed into the hands of the South Vietnamese.

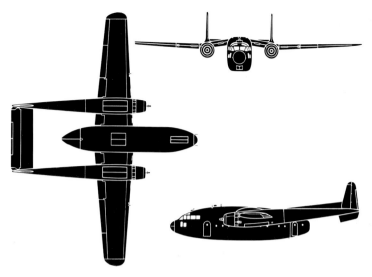

Above: Three-view of original C-119G Flying Boxcar cargo model.

Burdened with the weight of guns, ammunition, and other equipment, which permitted it to operate only at low altitude, the G model gunship did not venture among the mountains of southern Laos, where hostile gunners waited in the darkness. Against the anti-aircraft defenses of the Ho Chi Minh Trail, the Air Force used the AC-119K, featuring pod-mounted jet auxiliary engines, a pair of 20mm cannon in addition to the four machine guns, and both radar and an infrared sensor to locate the enemy. A squadron of these Stinger gunships flown by members of the Air Force Reserve mobilized as a result of the Tet offensive, entered combat shortly after the Shadows. Gradually the enemy 37mm and 57mm gun crews protecting the roads and trails in southern Laos became too numerous and too accurate for the Stinger to patrol such vital areas as the transportation and storage complex around Tchepone.

In the hands of South Vietnamese airmen, neither the Shadow nor the Stinger could successfully challenge enemy infiltrators. During the bloody truce that prevailed from January 1973 until the 1975 North Vietnamese invasion, supplies and reinforcements moved freely through Laos.

Below left: Interior of an early AC-119G Shadow newly arrived in South Vietnam on 8 January 1969, showing fixed SUU-11 gun pods.

Below: The AC-119G Shadow had no J85 booster jet pods.

Fairchild C-123 Provider

C-123B, K, UC-123B, AC-123B.

Origin: Fairchild Hiller.
Type: Transport, night attack system.
Engines: Two 2,300hp Pratt & Whitney R-2800-99W radials; (C-123K) the two piston engines plus two 2,850lb (1293kg) thrust General Electric J85-GE-17 auxiliary turbojets mounted in underwing pods.
Dimensions: Span 110ft (33·35m); length 75ft 3in (23·25m); height 34ft 1in (10·38m).
Weight: (B) empty 31,058lb (14,000kg); maximum gross weight 60,000lb (27,240kg); (K) empty 35,336lb (16,042kg); maximum takeoff weight 60,000lb (27,240kg).
Performance: (B) maximum speed 245mph (392km/h); cruising speed 190mph (304km/h); (K) maximum speed at 10,000ft (3050m) 228mph (367km/h); cruising speed at 10,000ft (3050m) 173mph (278km/h).
Armament: (AC-123B) bomb canister dispenser.
Flight crew: (Transports and UC-123B) four.
History: Based on an all-metal glider designed by Chase Aircraft and intended for conversion into a powered assault transport, the Fairchild C-123B prototype first flew on 1 September 1954; the K model made its first flight on 27 May 1966.
Users: US Air Force Tactical Air Command, PACAF (C-123B, K, UC-123B, AC-123B); South Vietnamese Air Force (C-123B, K). ▶

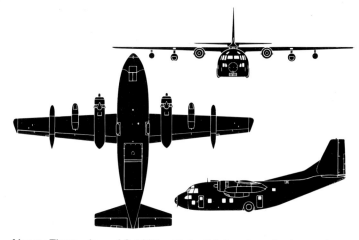

Above: Three-view of C-123K with both jet pods and pylon tanks.

Below: Hectic activity in 1970 as Vietnamese troops, civilians and cargo are assembled for airlift by C-123B. The location is not identified but could be Tan Son Nhut AB, HQ of the ALCC (Airlift Control Center).

▶**Tactical employment:** In the hands of a group of airmen who called themselves The Mule Train, the C-123B became the first US Air Force transport to see service in South Vietnam. Before the United States became involved in the war in Southeast Asia, the Provider had undergone various modifications. A wider undercarriage, for instance, helped correct a sensitivity to cross winds during landings. Also, ten of the B models received wingtip auxiliary jet engines for service in the Arctic, a change that foreshadowed the addition of underwing turbojets for operations during the conflict.

The Providers flown by The Mule Train soon were joined by the UC-123Bs of Project Ranch Hand, which sprayed pesticides for malaria prevention and herbicides that destroyed both the forest that concealed the Viet Cong and the rice and manioc plant that fed them. In time of crisis, such as the enemy's Tet offensive early in 1968, or following the cancellation of

Above: RAAF Caribou crew disembarking from an unpainted C-123B after a Vietnam familiarization trip in August 1964.

Below left: Vietnamese paratroops on combat mission from C-123s.

Below right: The C-123 Provider was the chief defoliant aircraft used in Vietnam; these came from the 12th Air Commando Squadron.

herbicide operations, mechanics removed the tanks from the spray planes, which then functioned as ordinary C-123Bs, carrying troops and cargo.

Like most other transports, the C-123B demonstrated its versatility during the Vietnam fighting. One served as personal transport for General William C. Westmoreland, commander of the US Military Assistance Command, Vietnam. Two others, unofficially called AC-123s, mounted a sensor capable of detecting enemy trucks. Upon locating an enemy truck convoy, the night attack model dropped canisters that opened to scatter small, spherical bomblets.

The C-123 also dispensed flares to illuminate targets for fighters or tactical bombers. Nicknamed Candlestick when carrying out this role, the plane proved effective against truck traffic in Laos, except in those areas where the anti-aircraft defenses had become too formidable.

The addition of jet auxiliary engines scarcely affected the Provider's speed, but the greater power improved performance in other ways. The C-123K could, for example, climb at 1,220 feet (372 meters) per minute with one piston engine shut down and in that same condition maintain level flight at an altitude of 21,000 feet (6·430 meters). Also, the K model could clear a fifty-foot (15-meter) obstacle after a takeoff run of just 1,809 feet (551 meters).

This boost in performance could mean the difference between life and death for those on board the plane. During the encirclement of Khe Sanh early in 1968, the Ks touched down, unloaded, took on wounded or other passengers, and took off again within one minute, giving North Vietnamese mortar crews the most fleeting of targets. In May of that year, one of these aircraft, piloted by Lt. Col. Joe M. Jackson, landed on the debris-strewn runway at Kham Duc to pick up the members of an Air Force airlift control team, the last of the base's defenders, and take off despite enemy rocket and small arms fire.

The C-123Bs and Ks figured in Vietnamization, the effort to equip and train the South Vietnamese to defend themselves. Originally, the Provider was to have been the mainstay of a tactical airlift fleet that included C-47s and C-119Gs. However, in a last minute effort to strengthen this element of South Vietnam's air arm, the United States added de Havilland C-7As and a few Lockheed C-130As.

Below: A C-123B on an airdrop over the Central Highlands; they made 105 para-drops and 179 landings at Khe Sanh in early 1968.

General Dynamics F-111

F-111A.

Origin: General Dynamics/Fort Worth Division.
Type: Two-seat, all-weather tactical fighter/bomber.
Engines: Two Pratt and Whitney TF30 turbofan engines, each giving approximately 20,000lb (9072kg) thrust.
Dimensions: (A) Wing Span 63ft (19·20m); fully swept 31ft 11·4in (9·74m); length 73ft 6in (22·40m); height 17ft 1·4in (5·22m).
Weight: Empty (A) 46,172lb (20,943kg); maximum loaded (A) 91,500lb (41,500kg).
Performance: Maximum speed (clean) Mach 2·2 at 35,000ft or nearly 1,450mph (2335km/h); maximum speed at low level (clean) Mach 1·2 or 800mph (1237km/h); range, with maximum internal fuel, over 3,300nm (3,795 miles) (6,106km).
Armament: Normally (in SE Asia) 24 bombs of 500 or 750lb (227 or 340kg).
History: (A) first flight 21 December 1964, production aircraft 12 February 1967, SE Asia deployment 15 March 1968.
User: US Air Force, Tactical Air Command, PACAF.

Tactical employment: During the early 1960s the US Air Force foresaw a need for a new tactical fighter that could take off and land on a runway of less than 3,000 feet (915m), retain a low level radius including a route of 400 miles (644km) at Mach 1·2, and deliver conventional or nuclear weapons as well as negotiate a 1,000lb (453kg) internal payload, un-refueled over a 3,300nm (3,795 miles, 6106km) route. To obtain this performance, engineers recalled earlier experiments by Bell Aircraft and Grumman, designing a pivoting wing. For takeoffs and landings, the wing formed a right angle to the fuselage; at supersonic speed, the wing was swept sharply back. From the beginning the aircraft (F-111A) was plagued with engine and weight problems. Indeed, the final weight of the aircraft was 20,000lb (13,636kg) heavier than the Office of the Secretary of Defense (OSD) had envisioned.

However, the aircraft's successful performance in Combat Bullseye I testing in early 1967 convinced the Air Force that the F-111A was ready for combat. The F-111 conducted night and all-weather attacks against North

Below: F-111A 67-113 on last mission from Takhli, 15 August 1973.

Above: F-111As on their second (1972-73) deployment at Takhli, when they pioneered the use of electronically capable terrain-following attack aircraft to strike any target blind in any weather.

Vietnam during Operation Combat Lancer in March 1968. In the first 55 missions, two aircraft were lost, and a third went down less than a month later, causing the Air Force to suspend further use of the airplane for a limited period to investigate the cause of the losses and make any necessary modifications. After the plane returned to the air, the crashes resumed. When the 15th F-111 went down on 22 December 1969 because of failure of the forged wing pivot fitting, the Air Force ordered all F-111s grounded, and the plane did not return to service until the following July.

In September 1972 F-111As were returned to Southeast Asia where they saw action in North Vietnam as well as in Laos. On 8 November F-111As flew some 20 strikes over North Vietnam in weather so severe that all other aircraft were grounded. Yet, despite its fine showing, trouble persisted. The F-111s experienced engine malfunctioning, internal navigation weapons release difficulties, shortages of spare parts, and problems with the terrain following radar (TFR). In spite of these nagging and disappointing problems the F-111s flew nearly 3,000 missions in Vietnam before the Paris peace accords were signed in January 1973. Included in these activities were night attacks on surface-to-air missile sites during the Linebacker II operations (December 1972 to January 1973).

Grumman A-6

A-6A, B, E, KA-6D, EA-6A Intruders; EA-6B Prowler.

Origin: Grumman Aerospace.
Type: (A-6A) two place all weather, low-altitude, carrier-based attack plane; (B) similar to A-6A except configured for Standard ARM missile; A-6E configuration has provisions for a forward-looking infrared sensor and laser detection and ranging; (KA-6D) aerial tanker based on A-6A; (EA-6B) four-place electronic warfare platform.
Engines: Two 9,300lb (4281kg) thrust Pratt and Whitney J52-8A axial flow turbojets; (EA-6B) two 11,200lb (5080kg) J52-408.
Dimensions: Span 53ft (16·15m); length (A-6A) 54ft 7in (16·64m); (EA-6A) 55ft 3in (16·84m); (EA-6B) 59ft 5in (18·11m); height (A-6A) 15ft 7in (4·75m); (EA-6A, B) 16ft 3in (4·95m).
Weight: Empty (A-6A) 25,684lb (11,650kg); (EA-6A) 27,769lb (12,596kg); (EA-6B) 34,581lb (15,686kg); maximum loaded (A-6A) 60,626lb (27,500kg); (EA-6A) 56,500lb (25,628kg); (EA-6B) 58,500lb (26,535kg).
Performance: Maximum speed (clean A-6A) 685mph (1102km/h) at sea level or 625mph (1006km/h, Mach 0·94) at height; (EA-6B) 599mph (998km/h) at sea level; service ceiling (A-6A) 41,660ft (12,700m); (EA-6B) 39,000ft (11,582m); ferry range (A-6A) 3,225 miles (5190km); (EA-6A) 2,995 miles (4820km).
Armament: (Except KA-6D and EA-6B) five stores locations each rated at 3,600lb (1633kg) with maximum total load of 15,000lb (6804kg); typical load, thirty 500lb (227kg) bombs; (EA-6B) none.
History: First flight (YA2F-1) 19 April 1960; service acceptance of A-6A 1 February 1963; first flight (EA-6A) 1963, (EA-6B) 25 May 1968.
User: US Navy and Marine Corps.

Tactical employment: The KA-6A served as a tanker in Southeast Asia, and the EA-6As flew electronic warfare missions, including radar destruction or suppression, for the US Marine Corps. The primary missions of the A-6A were close-air-support, all-weather and night attacks on enemy troop concentrations, and night interdiction. The A-6 Intruder first saw combat in July 1965 when aircraft of VA-75 from the USS *Independence* hit targets in North Vietnam. During the course of the war, this plane flew most of its missions from the decks of Navy attack carriers of the Seventh Fleet, but Marine Corps squadrons at Da Nang and Chu Lai also used the Intruder.

During 1966, while some A-6s were blasting North Vietnamese truck convoys bound for South Vietnam by way of Laos, Intruders from VA-65 of the *Constellation* were bombing fuel storage sites that kept the trucks rolling. In July, for instance, two Navy A-6s attacked the Yen Hau petroleum storage depot south of Vinh raising a pillar of smoke visible some sixty miles (96km) from the target.

Below: Most A-6 missions were attacks from minimum safe altitude but these A-6As from USS *Constellation* were on level bombing.

Above: Another *Constellation* A-6A with 22 Snakeye retarded bombs.

A single A-6 was responsible for destroying the Hai Duong bridge, a major link between Haiphong and Hanoi. The crew from VA-65 caught the North Vietnamese off guard in a highly defended area. Using live 2,000lb (909kg) bombs, the elusive Intruder obliterated the center span.

On the night of 30 October 1967 one A-6A performed one of the most difficult single-plane strikes of the war. Launched to attack the Hanoi railroad ferry slip, the plane flown by Commander Charles B. Hunter carried eighteen 500 pound (226kg) bombs. He made a low-level, instrument approach, picking his way through limestone karst formations near the Red River Valley. As he drew clear of the limestone outcroppings Hunter began picking up enemy radar impulses, and as he approached the ferry slip, he saw the first of 16 SAMs that would be fired at him that night. As the missile got overhead it dived directly toward his aircraft. Instead of jettisoning his 9,000lbs (4077kg) of bombs he executed a high "G" barrel-roll to port, an exceedingly dangerous maneuver at low altitude. The SAM exploded within 200 feet (under 61m) of the plane, leaving it shaken but undamaged.

As Hunter began the actual bombing run his Intruder had to evade an antiaircraft barrage, as well as five missiles. To avoid the SAMs he flew at deck level, and each one exploded some 400 feet (122m) above him, flooding the cockpit with an orange light. Despite flak, SAMs, and search lights, the A-6 bored in and released its bombs whereupon Hunter made a seven "G" turn to starboard. As he turned away he could see the string of bombs falling on the designated target. Missions like this caused Vice Admiral William F. Bringle, Commander Seventh Fleet, to state that: "The low-level night missions flown by the A-6 over Hanoi and Haiphong were among the most demanding missions we have ever asked our aircrews to fly. Fortunately, there is an abundance of talent, courage, and aggressive leadership in these A-6 squadrons."

Like the EA-6A, the EA-6B Prowler waged electronic warfare. The B model's stretched fuselage accommodated two countermeasures technicians. Besides possessing greater jamming ability, the Prowler carried a chin-mounted infrared sensor to help the crew locate targets.

Grumman F8F

F8F-1, -1B.

Origin: Grumman Aircraft Engineering Corporation.
Type: Single-seat tactical fighter.
Engine: One 2,210hp Pratt & Whitney R-2800 34 W eighteen-cylinder two-row radial air-cooled.
Dimensions: Span 35ft 6in (10·82m); width folded 23ft 9½in (7·25m); length 27ft 6in (8·38m); height 13ft 10in (4·22m).
Performance: Maximum speed over 455mph (732km/h); speed at sea level 425mph (684km/h); service ceiling 42,000ft (12,895m); normal range with drop tank 1,650 miles (2640km); maximum ferrying range 2,200 miles (3740km).
Weight: Loaded 9,300lb (4222kg); wing loading 39·3lb/sq ft (191·7 kg/m²); power loading at take-off 4·5lb/hp (2·0kg/hp).
Armament: Four ·50 caliber (12·7mm) machine-guns (F8F-1), or four 20mm cannon (F8F-1B mounted two in each wing outside airscrew disc). Provision for bombs up to total of 2,000lb (907kg) or four 5in (12·7cm) rocket projectiles under wings.
History: First flight (XF8F-1) 21 August 1944; production contracts placed 6 October 1944; first deliveries February 1945.
User: French Air Force.

Tactical employment: The French Air Force used the F8F-1 principally for attacking Viet Minh troops. The four 20mm cannon of the F8F-1B proved deadly against men on the ground as did the napalm and rockets that both models carried. Bearcats fought in all of the important battles from Nghia to Dien Bien Phu, sometimes operating from airstrips inside the fortified camps. During the fight for Dien Bien Phu in 1954 Bearcats attacked enemy supply lines and tried unsuccessfuly to silence the 170 or more enemy antiaircraft guns that ringed the base. A few of these planes, fitted with cameras, flew reconnaissance missions, recording among other things the Viet Minh encirclement and eventual conquest of Dien Bien Phu.

Right: F8F-1B Bearcats of the Armée de l'Air operating from Bac Mai early in the Indo-China war in September 1952.

Below: A mix of F8F-1 and F8F-1B Bearcats of the Armée de l'Air warming up for a mission from Dien Bien Phu on 10 January 1954.

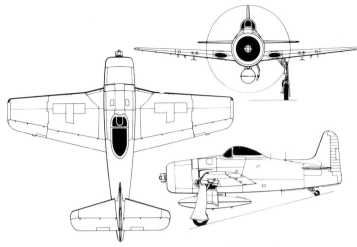

Above: Three-view of F8F-1 with centreline drop tank.

Grumman HU-16 Albatross

HU-16B.

Origin: Grumman Aircraft Engineering Corporation.
Type: Rescue amphibian.
Engine: Two 1,425hp Wright R-1820-76A or -76B radials.
Dimensions: Span 96ft 8in (29·46m); length 62ft 10in (19·18m); height 25ft 10in (7·87m).
Weight: Empty 22,883lb (10,380kg); normal loaded weight 30,353lb (13,768kg); maximum loaded weight 37,500lb (17,010kg).
Performance: Maximum speed 236mph (379km/h); maximum cruising speed 224mph (362km/h); range with maximum fuel 2,850 miles (4587km).
Armament: None.
Flight crew: Five.
History: Prototype first flight October 1947; first production model entered military service July 1949; first flight HU-16B 16 January 1956.
User: US Air Force Military Airlift Command, Aerospace Rescue and Recovery Service.

Tactical employment: In June 1964, the first HU-16Bs arrived at Da Nang, South Vietnam, to begin flying rescue missions over the Gulf of Tonkin. At the time, the only other rescue craft serving in Southeast Asia was the short-range HH-43 helicopter. By the end of 1965, the Albatross had landed at sea to rescue sixty downed airmen. Besides recovering crews from coastal waters, sometimes racing North Vietnamese junks to the life raft that was keeping an aviator afloat, the HU-16B functioned as a radio relay station during rescue operations.

Development of the HH-3E helicopter, which could refuel from the HC-130 rescue control aircraft, signalled the end of the Albatross. Thanks to its ability to refuel from the Hercules, the helicopter could remain on station as long as the Grumman amphibian and recover a downed flier while hovering above him, without risking a landing and takeoff in the open sea.

Below: One of the HU-16B Albatross rescue amphibians parked at Da Nang AB in theatre paint scheme in April 1966.

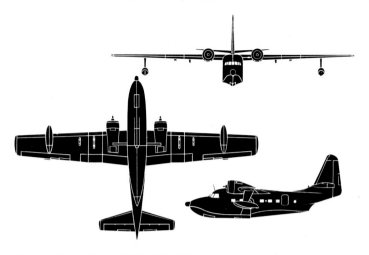

Above: Three-view of HU-16B without external tanks.

Below: HU-16B 51-7163, uncamouflaged but with 10-year O-prefix.

Grumman OV-1 Mohawk

OV-1A, B, C.

Origin: Grumman Aerospace.
Type: Two-place battlefield surveillance craft.
Engine: Two 1,100hp Lycoming T53-L-15 turboprops.
Dimensions: Span (OV-1A, C) 42ft (12·8m), (OV-1B) 48ft (14·63m); length 41ft (12·5m); height 12ft 8in (3·86m).
Weight: Empty, fully equipped (A) 9,937lb (4507kg), (B) 11,067lb (5020kg), (C) 10,400lb (4717kg); normal takeoff weight (A) 12,672lb (5748kg), (B) 13,650lb (6197kg), (C) 13,040lb (5915kg).
Performance: Maximum speed at 5,000ft (1520m) (A, C) 308mph (496km/h), (B) 297mph (478km/h); maximum cruising speed (A) 304mph (489km/h), (B) 275mph (443km/h), (C) 297mph (478km/h); maximum range with external tanks (A) 1,410 miles (2270km), (B) 1,230 miles (1980km), (C) 1,330 miles (2140km).
Armament: None (but see text).
History: First flight 14 April 1959; entered service in South Vietnam July 1962.
User: US Army.

Tactical employment: Grumman designed the Mohawk as a battlefield reconnaissance plane for the US Army and Marine Corps. Although the marines withdrew from the development program, the Army accepted and evaluated nine of the planes and found them so impressive that it ordered three basic types—the OV-1A, B, and C.

Fitted with a panoramic camera capable of horizon-to-horizon coverage, the OV-1A (redesignated from OA-1A in 1962) flew photo reconnaissance missions in South Vietnam. The plane obtained aerial views of small targets—hill masses, road junctions, or hamlets—in the kind of detail needed by ground commanders. Early in the war, crews mounted guns on a few of these aircraft, but the modification did not become standard.

The OV-1B mounted side-looking airborne radar, housed in a long pod beneath the forward part of the fuselage. Although remaining over South Vietnamese territory, this model could maintain nighttime radar surveillance over roads in southern Laos, detecting targets for Air Force gunships or fighter-bombers. The equipment scanned on either side of the aircraft, fashioning a radar map that could be reproduced photographically while the Mohawk was in flight.

Instead of using radar, the OV-1C maintained surveillance over the battlefields of South Vietnam with infrared detection equipment and a forward-aimed camera. Because the North Vietnamese and Viet Cong relied so heavily upon darkness to conceal their activity, the infrared sensor proved especially valuable.

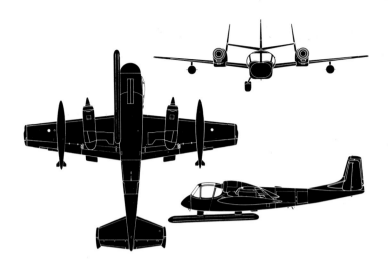

Above: Three-view of Grumman OV-1B (plan shows underside).

In 1967, Grumman converted four C models into OV-1D prototypes, using 1,150hp Lycoming T53-L-701 turboprop engines and mounting all three kinds of sensors—cameras, side-looking radar, and infrared detection gear. The Army promptly ordered 37 of the Ds.

Above: Although not standard, many Mohawks in Southeast Asia carried various weapons.

Below: OV-1B Mohawk (possibly 23rd Special Warfare Aviation Detachment, US Army, Vietnam.

Hughes OH-6A Cayuse

OH-6A.

Origin: Hughes Helicopters, Division of Summa Corporation.
Type: Light observation helicopter.
Engines: One 317shp Allison T63-A-5A turboshaft.
Dimensions: Main (4-blade) rotor diameter 26ft 4in (8·03m); fuselage length 23ft (7·01m); height 8ft 1½in (2·48m).
Weight: Empty 1,146lb (520kg); gross 2,400lb (1090kg); payload 930lb (422kg).
Performance: Maximum speed 150mph (241km/h); normal range at 5,000ft (1500m) 380 miles (611km).
Armament: Provision for carrying XM-27 7·62mm machine gun with 2,000 to 4,000 rounds per minute capacity, or XM-75 grenade launcher.
Accommodation: Two crew, four passengers.
History: First flight 27 February 1963; first delivery 1966.
User: US Army.

Tactical employment: The US Defense Department envisioned a single helicopter to perform such duties as personnel or cargo transport, light ground attack or casualty evacuation, observation, and photographic reconnaissance. The OH-6 was the result but in South Vietnam the Cayuse proved most effective at visual reconnaissance, searching out signs of the enemy even in heavily defended areas like the A Shau Valley. The light helicopter skimmed the treetops, its crew peering through gaps in the jungle canopy in search of tracks, cooking fires, huts, or other signs of the enemy.

The OH-6A observation helicopter joined with the AH-1G Cobra gunship as "Pink Teams" to screen the deployment of air cavalry troops. These Pink Teams proved their worth as requirements mounted to support more and more operations and an ever larger area.

In August 1970 the First Cavalry conducted an analysis of the productivity of its aircraft assets. The analysis disclosed that an airlift escort by two Cobra gunships was the division's least productive mission. It was determined that the escort could be foregone since gunships were almost always available at the pickup and landing zones. Also, the general support

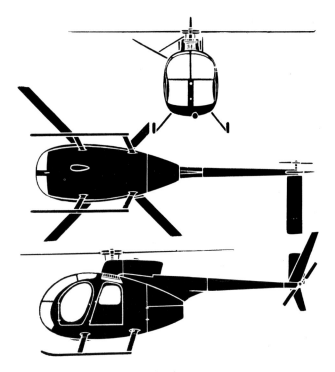

Above: Three-view of basic OH-6A without any external kit.

missions normally flown by the OH-6A could be supported by fewer aircraft if carefully controlled. Consequently, two provisional air cavalry troops were formed attaching OH-6As to assault weapons companies. This enlarged the air cavalry squadron to five troops and greatly increased its ability to cover its far-flung operations.

Left: Instrument check flight by crew of 34th General Support Gp, Tan Son Nhut, October 1967.

Kaman HH-43 Huskie

HH-43A, HH-43B, HH-43F.

Origin: Kaman Aircraft Corporation.
Type: Crash rescue helicopter.
Engines: (HH-43B) One 860shp Lycoming T53-L-1B turboshaft.
Dimensions: (HH-43B) Main rotor diameter 47ft (14·33m); fuselage length 25ft 2in (7·67m); height 12ft 7in (3·84m).
Weight: (HH-43B) Empty 4,469lb (2027kg); normal takeoff 5,969lb (2708kg); maximum takeoff 9,150lb (4150kg).
Performance: (HH-43B) Maximum level speed at sea level 120mph (193km/h); range at 5,000ft (1525m) no allowances 277 miles (445km).
Armament: None.
Accommodation: (HH-43B) Two crew, six passengers.
History: (HH-43B) First flight December 1958.
User: US Air Force, Aerospace Rescue and Recovery Service.

Tactical employment: In the early 1960s the HH-43, a short-range (220 mile, 354km) helicopter, was the only crash rescue helicopter in the US Air Force inventory. Local base rescue units in the United States and overseas which operated the HH-43 considered the Huskie inadequate for Southeast Asia duty.

Below: Scramble of an HH-43F of the 38th Air Rescue and Recovery Squadron to cover emergency landing at Da Nang in May 1967.

Above: Three-view of HH-43B (HH-43F very similar).

Above: Winching down Air Rescue crewman into jungle during recovery by Jungle Penetrator of wounded troops.

By default, however, the Air Force had to depend either on the Huskie or the equally inadequate Army and Marine Corps helicopters. In March 1964 three HH-43 units were transferred to Southeast Asia from the Philippines and Okinawa. In June 1964 two HH-43 companies including 36 personnel on temporary duty were deployed to Nakhon Phanom, Thailand. On 20 October Detachment 4 of Pacific Air Rescue Center, equipped with three HH-43Fs, arrived at Bien Hoa. These modified HH-43s possessed heavy armor plating to protect their crews from hostile fire and a 250-foot (76·2m) long cable to facilitate rescues in the high rain forest.

By January 1966 the Air Force had activated the 3rd Aerospace Rescue and Recovery Group at Tan Son Nhut to serve as the primary rescue agency in Southeast Asia. Besides the HH-43s at Nakhon Phanom and Bien Hoa, the Air Force employed HU-16 amphibians to rescue pilots downed at sea. A total of ten rescue detachments were based throughout South Vietnam and four in Thailand. To extend their operations, rescue crews sought out clearings in the jungle, or remote mountain tops where they could stockpile fuel to await calls for help. The air rescue groups also installed extra fuel tanks in the helicopters and carried either 150-gallon (682 l) containers, or 55-gallon (250 l) drums. They could land en route to the objective and top off (fill up) the fuel supply.

Kaman UH-2 Seasprite

UH-2A, UH-2B, UH-2C.

Origin: Kaman Aircraft Corporation.
Type: Twin-engine general purpose helicopter. All UH-2A/B were converted to the twin-engine configuration and designated UH-2C.
Engines: Two 1,250shp General Electric T58-GE-8F turboshaft.
Dimensions: Main rotor diameter 44ft (13·41m); fuselage length 41ft (12·50m); height 13ft 6¼in (4·12m).
Weight: Empty 7,390lb (3351kg); takeoff 9,951lb (4514kg); maximum 11,614lb (5268kg).
Performance: Maximum level speed at sea level 157mph (252kmh); normal range 425 miles (685km).
Armament: TAT-102A turret system with 7·62mm Minigun.
Accommodation: Two crew, 11 passengers, or 4 litters.
History: First flight 2 July 1959. UH-2A entered US Navy service on 18 December 1962 (88 were built). UH-2B entered shipboard service on 8 August 1963 (102 built). UH-2C deliveries began in August 1967.
User: US Navy.

Tactical employment: Winner of a 1956 US Navy competition for a fast, long-range utility helicopter, the Seasprite was in production from 1961–1966. The Kaman design replaced earlier piston engine helicopters for a variety of tasks, including reconnaissance, supply, carrier "plane guard", communications, ship-to-shore transport and casualty evacuation. However, its principal role remained search and rescue.

The first UH-2A deliveries were made to the US Navy's squadron HU-2 in December 1962 and first shipped to sea aboard the USS *Independence* in June 1963. Two months later the UH-2B was also assigned to the USS *Albany*. Both types were used extensively in Southeast Asia.

In March 1965 Kaman Aircraft completed a conversion program to

Above: Three-view of final SH-2F with external loads.

install two T58-GE-8 engines in pods on either side of the rotor pylon to improve the Seasprite's performance. Starting in 1967 UH-2As and UH-2Bs were converted to UH-2Cs. About one hundred such conversions were completed by the spring of 1968.

The US Army acquired a small batch of UH-2s and named the aircraft Tomahawk. One aircraft was fitted with a 1,500shp T58-GE-10 engine and evaluated in the ground support role, with an M-6 four-gun turret in the nose and launching pylons on the cabin sides for Minigun pods, 40mm grenade launchers, pods of unguided rockets, or anti-tank missiles.

Below left: an armoured HH-2C with four-bladed tail rotor and chin-turret 7·62mm Minigun system.

Below: A UH-2C with twin engines and three-blade tail rotor landing on the deck of USS *Coral Sea*.

Lockheed C-5 Galaxy

C-5A

Origin: Lockheed-Georgia.
Type: Transport.
Engines: Four 41,000lb (18,600kg) thrust General Electric TF39-GE-1 turbofans.
Dimensions: Span 222ft 8½in (67·88m); length 247ft 10in (75·54m); height 65ft 1½in (19·85m).
Weight: Basic operating weight 325,244lb (147,528kg); design payload 265,000lb (120,000kg); maximum takeoff weight 764,500lb (346,770kg).
Performance: Maximum speed 571mph (919km/h) at 25,000ft (6500m); maximum cruising speed 537mph (864km/h) at 30,000ft (9000m); range 6,500 miles (10,460m) with maximum fuel and a payload of 80,000lb (36,287kg).
Armament: None.
Flight crew: Seven.
History: First flight 30 June 1968; deliveries of production models began on 17 December 1969; flights between the United States and South Vietnam commenced the following year.
User: US Air Force Military Airlift Command.

Tactical employment: Design studies for the Galaxy began in 1963 as Lockheed engineers and Air Force program managers fashioned an airplane capable of carrying "outsize" cargo, such as tanks or trucks, while taking off from an 8,000ft (2440m) runway or landing on a forward airstrip as short as 4,000ft (1220m). In its vast interior, the C-5A had two decks, the lower able to accommodate 270 troops and the upper an additional 75 soldiers, plus the five-man flight crew, and 15 relief crewmen or special passengers. Rather than men, the Galaxy normally carried cargo — a pair of main battle tanks, for example, or 16 light trucks — that had boarded either over a ramp at the rear of the transport or through the hinged nose. Its stowage capacity proved especially valuable in rushing armor, helicopters, and artillery to South Vietnam during the hectic time between the North Vietnamese invasion of the South in March 1972 and the signing of a ceasefire in January 1973.

The C-5A also took part in the airlift that immediately preceded the fall of South Vietnam. On 4 April 1975, while evacuating some 250 South Vietnam orphans and American civilians from beleaguered Saigon, a Galaxy began losing cabin pressure. The rear cargo doors failed, decompression hurled some of the children and other passengers from the rear deck, and the plane crashed out of control. A total of 172 persons died as a result of the accident.

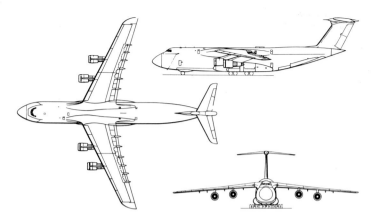

Above: Three-view of C-5A Galaxy (note landing gear in front view).

Above: Off-loading CH-47 from C-5A of 437th MAW, Cam Ranh Bay.

Below: C-5A downloading cargo at Cam Ranh Bay, July 1970.

Lockheed C-130 Hercules

C-130A, B, E; DC-130A, E; KC-130F; HC-130P;

Origin: Lockheed-Georgia.

Type: Transport, tanker, gunship, drone controller, airborne battlefield command and control center, weather reconnaissance craft, electronic reconnaissance platform; search, rescue, and recovery craft.

Engines: (C-130A and variants) four Allison 3,750hp T56A-1A or -9 turboprops turning three-blade propellers; (HC-130P) four Allison 4,910hp T56A-15 turboprops turning four-blade propellers; (all others) four Allison 4,050hp T56A-7 turboprops turning four-blade propellers.

Dimensions: Span 132ft 7in (40·25m); length 97ft 9in (29.78m); (HC-130P) 106ft 4in (30.10m) with Fulton recovery system extended; height 38ft 3in (11·7m).

Weight: Empty (C-130A) 63,000lb (28,576kg), (C-130B) 63,300lb (31,460kg), (C-130E) 72,892lb (33,063kg); maximum payload (C-130A) 36,600lb (16,600kg), (C-130B) 35,700lb (16,193kg), (C-130E) 45,000lb (20,412kg).

Performance: Maximum cruising speed (C-130A) 356mph (573km/h), (C-130B) 367mph (590km/h), (C-130E) 368mph (592km/h); range with maximum payload (C-130A) 1,830 miles (2945km) at 335mph (539km/h), (C-130B) 2,300 miles (3700km) at 340mph (547km/h), (C-130E) 2,420 miles (3895km).

Armament: (AC-130A Gunship II) four 20mm and four 7·62mm guns; (AC-130A Surprise Package, Pave Pronto and AC-130E Spectre) two 40mm, two 20mm, and two 7·62mm guns; (AC-130H Pave Aegis) one 105mm howitzer, one 40mm, two 20mm, and two 7·62mm guns.

Flight crew: (Transport versions) five; (gunships) 10 to 14.

History: The prototype flew for the first time in August 1954. The C-130A, first flown on 7 April 1955, remained in production from December 1956

Right: Several forms of extraction system were used by the C-130 for delivery of cargo without landing. Here a cargo pallet is pulled out by four parachutes (the more common LAPES, low-altitude parachute extraction system, uses a single 22ft (6·7m) ring-slot canopy, not a group of four). Another method used in Vietnam was the GPES, pictured on page 87. The chief advantage of the parachute extraction technique was that it could be used anywhere the aircraft could make a really low run. No ground equipment was necessary but great skill was.

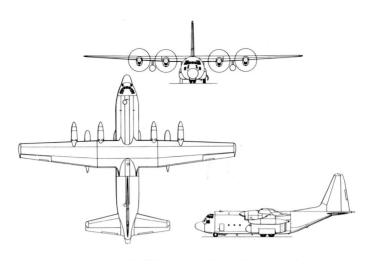

Above: Three-view of C-130 cargo model with external tanks.

to February 1959. The B model, featuring greater fuel capacity, more power-ful engines, and four-blade propellers entered service in June 1959. Production of the C-130E, fitted with underwing fuel tanks, began in April 1962.

Users: US Air Force Tactical Air Command, PACAF (WC-130B, E) Air Weather Service; (HC-130P) Aerospace Rescue and Recovery Service; (KC-130F) US Marine Corps; (C-130A) South Vietnamese Air Force.

Tactical employment: In the hands of the "trash haulers", as the crews of Tactical Air Command transports styled themselves, the Lockheed C-130▶

▶proved the most valuable airlift instrument in the Southeast Asia conflict, so valuable that General William W. Momyer, Seventh Air Force commander, refused for a time to let them land at Khe Sanh where the airstrip was under fire from North Vietnamese troops surrounding that base.

Fitted with an air-conditioned capsule containing electronic gear and data processing equipment, the C-130 became an airborne battlefield command and control center, from which officers directed air strikes, matching ordnance with targets and ensuring an orderly flow of aircraft. The addition of other electronic gear enabled the C-130B to relay friendly radio signals or to record enemy transmissions.

Another task undertaken by the Hercules was that of drone controller. DC-130As or Es launched Ryan-Teledyne reconnaissance drones and guided them across heavily defended areas judged too dangerous for manned reconnaissance craft. At the end of the mission, a helicopter snagged the parachute that was lowering the drone earthward, thus recovering the vehicle and the data it had collected.

The Air Weather Service of the US Air Force used some of its WC-130s as rainmakers over southern Laos. By scattering pellets of lead iodide or silver iodide, the planes tried to intensify the seasonal monsoon rains and disrupt truck traffic through this region. Also to hamper the passage of supply vehicles, C-130s dumped chemicals that were supposed to destroy the stability of the soil and turn roads into bogs. In neither case were the results worthwhile.

The HC-130P served as a command and control center for search and rescue operations — and for the 1975 attack upon Koh Tang island after the Cambodian seizure of the cargo ship *Mayaguez* — coordinating the efforts of helicopters and their escorting attack planes or fighter-bombers. This Hercules variant carried pod-shaped underwing fuel tanks with probe-and-drogue refueling equipment compatible with rescue helicopters like the HH-3E. Mounted at the nose of the P model was the retractable yoke used with the Fulton recovery system to engage a nylon line sent aloft with a balloon and snatch an individual, wearing a harness attached to the line, into the air.

The KC-130F, flown by the US Marine Corps, traced its origin to a pair of C-130As borrowed from the Air Force and modified for probe-and-drogue

Left: Daytime flight test for an AC-130H. This model usually flew its combat missions at night, for which purpose it was liberally endowed with sensors and gun-aiming systems.

Above: Pallet delivery by GPES (ground proximity extraction system); this required a hook to catch a fixed installation.

refueling. Production models, based on the C-130B, carried 3,600 US gallons (13,620 liters) and could refuel two aircraft simultaneously. When the rubber fuel bladders had been removed from the cargo compartment, the plane served as a transport.

Bearing the nickname Blind Bat, C-130s served as fireships and forward air controllers, illuminating targets and directing strikes even in the fiercely defended region around Mu Gia Pass, which carried a main supply route from North Vietnam into Laos. In marking truck convoys or other targets, the Blind Bat had greater endurance and a shorter reaction time than the C-123 or C-47.

The most spectacular of all the modified C-130s were the gunships, which pierced the darkness using searchlights, flares, night observation▶

Above: AC-130H night gunship as used by USAF interdictor squadrons; all sensors and weapons faced to the left.

▶devices that intensified natural light, and a variety of electronic sensors such as radar, infrared equipment and even low-light-level television. On the various models, a computer automatically translated sensor data into instructions for the pilot, who kept his fixed, side-firing guns trained on target by adjusting the angle of bank as he circled. The earliest AC-130As carried eight multibarrel weapons, four of them 7·62mm and four 20mm. In the later A series and the longer range AC-130Es, two 40mm guns replaced two of the 20mm and two of the 7·62mm types. The AC-130H, converted from the C-130E, boasted a 105mm howitzer in lieu of one of the 40mm guns.

This evolution from many light weapons to fewer heavier ones resulted from the apparent need for more hitting power in the campaign against truck traffic. Although visual sightings and videotape film provided evidence of tens of thousands of trucks destroyed, reconnaissance flights could not locate the truck carcasses that should have littered the area. Concerned that trucks were being damaged rather than destroyed, the Air Force increased the AC-130 main battery from 20mm to 40mm and ultimately to a 105mm howitzer. Although it arrived too late to have much effect in southern Laos, the 105mm weapons proved deadly against enemy tanks and strongpoints during the North Vietnamese invasion of the South in 1972.

Top: Two fully armed A-4 Sky-hawk attack aircraft of Marine Air Group 12 are refuelled simultaneously at 10,000ft (3048m) by a KC-130F from VMGR-152, 1968.

Left: Takeoff by camou-flaged USAF C-130 from Khe Sanh air-strip in 1967.

Lockheed C-141 StarLifter

C-141A.

Origin: Lockheed-Georgia.
Type: Transport.
Engines: Four Pratt & Whitney TF-33P-7 turbofans, each developing 21,000lb (9525kg) thrust.
Dimensions: Span 159ft 11in (48·74m); length 145ft (44·2m); height 39ft 3½in (11·98m)
Weight: Empty 133,773lb (60,678kg); maximum payload 70,847lb (32,136kg); maximum 316,600lb (143,600kg).
Performance: Maximum speed 571mph (919km/h) at 25,000ft (7500m); economical cruising speed 495mph (797km/h); range with payload of 31,870lb (14,460kg) and maximum fuel capacity 6,140 miles (9880km).
Armament: None.
Flight crew: Six.
History: First flight 17 December 1963; first operational squadron April 1965; entered regular service between the United States and South Vietnam August 1965.
User: US Air Force Military Airlift Command.

Tactical employment: Developed as the aerial link in a world-wide materiel handling network, the C-141A carried up to 5,283 cubic feet of cargo, lashed to metal pallets loaded or unloaded by means of a ramp extending through doors at the rear of the cargo compartment. Besides delivering war materials to South Vietnam, the StarLifters flew reinforcements and replacements into the country and also took part in the troop withdrawals, part of the Vietnamization policy that began in the summer of 1969. The cargo area could accommodate 154 passengers. Fitted out as an aerial ambulance, the C-141A carried 80 litter patients and 16 seated passengers, usually a combination of walking wounded and medical attendants. Some medical evacuation flights followed a great circle route by way of Japan and Alaska to Andrews Air Force Base, Maryland, and the nearby Walter Reed Army Medical Center or Bethesda Naval Medical Center. Other C-141As crossed the Pacific via Guam and Hawaii, regularly carrying patients to an Air Force burn treatment center in Texas.

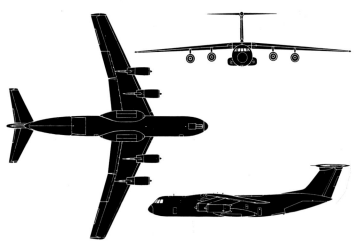

Above: Three-view of C-141A StarLifter (since converted to 141B).

Below: The C-141 was the chief strategic airlifter to SE Asia; here one unloads at Cam Ranh Bay AB, probably in 1967.

Left: Casualties are gently taken aboard a C-141A at Tan Son Nhut AB in January 1967 for aeromedical evacuation to California.

Lockheed EC-121 Warning Star

EC-121 D, R, T, C-121 C, G, J.

Origin: Lockheed Aircraft Corporation; Lockheed Aircraft Service Company (C-121J).
Type: Radar warning and fighter control aircraft (EC-121D, T), sensor relay aircraft (EC-121R), airborne television transmitter (C-121J), transport (C-121C, G).
Engines: Four 3,250hp Wright R-3350-34 or -91 Turbo-Compound radials.
Dimensions: (EC-121D) span 126ft 2in (37·95m); length 116ft 2in (35·41m); height 27ft (8·1m).
Weight: (EC-121D) empty 80,611lb (36,275kg); gross weight 143,600lb (64,620kg).
Performance: (EC-121D) maximum speed 321mph (517km/h) at 20,000ft (6100m); range 4,600 miles (7405km).
Armament: None.
Flight crew: (EC-121D) twenty-seven, including radar technicians.
History: Based on the Lockheed L-1049 Super Constellation commercial transport; first radar warning model was the RC-121C, which entered service in October 1953. In May of the following year the RC-121D (later re-designated EC-121D) made its appearance, its range increased over that of the C model by the addition of wingtip fuel tanks.
Users: US Air Force Aerospace Defense Command, Tactical Air Command, PACAF (EC-121 variants); Military Airlift Command and Air Force Reserve (C-121C, G); US Navy Oceanographic Air Survey Unit (C-121J).

Tactical employment: The US Air Force sent the EC-121D Warning Star—an official nickname that never supplanted Constellation or Connie among those who flew the type—to Southeast Asia to maintain radar surveillance over North Vietnam and sound the alarm if the Ilyushin Il-28 light bombers based there should launch an air attack against the South. The mission of the Constellations changed, however, and airborne radar operators soon began issuing warning of MiG attacks and alerting American pilots who were on the verge of straying over Chinese territory. The EC-121D and the improved EC-121T undertook still other missions, directing Air Force fighters into position to down MiGs, guiding fighters low on fuel to rendez-vous with aerial tankers, and plotting the positions of downed aircraft.

Shortly before the Rolling Thunder bombing of North Vietnam ended in 1968, the Tactical Air Command tried the EC-121 as an airborne command and control center for air operations over the North. Radar, computers, and visual displays on board the aircraft monitored attacks and enabled controllers to issue instructions based upon the defensive reactions.

Above: Warning Star O-23412, built as an RC-121D and in this photograph externally unchanged. Note DFC medal ribbon.

The EC-121R served as airborne relay for the electronic surveillance net emplaced in southern Laos to detect truck traffic on the Ho Chi Minh Trail. Sensors planted along roads were triggered by sound or movement and broadcast a radio signal relayed by the Constellation to a surveillance center at Nakhon Phanom, Thailand. At this facility, technicians plotted sensor activations to establish a pattern of enemy movement, and an operations section sometimes alerted patrolling aircraft to the location of truck convoys.

Unfortunately, the EC-121R soon became the weak link in the so-called Igloo White surveillance system. The plane was vulnerable to MiG attack, carried a large crew of trained specialists, and required spare parts that were becoming scarce. As a result, the Air Force tested a new relay aircraft, the QU-22, a radio controlled version of the Beechcraft Debonaire, a light plane designed for business use. The substitute did not live up to expectations, however, and could not replace the ageing Constellation.

Some C-121 transports saw service in Southeast Asia. Air Force Reserve and Military Airlift Command crews flew passengers across the Pacific in EC-121Cs and Gs. Navy airmen operated the C-121J, which served as an airborne radio and television transmitter for the armed forces network in South Vietnam. Taped or live broadcasts could originate on board this variant of the Constellation, nicknamed the Blue Eagle, or it could function as a relay station.

Below: A Navy Warning Star, probably an EC-121K from Fleet Air Recon Sqn 2 in October 1964. Some 25 aerials can be seen.

Lockheed P-2 Neptune

P-2E, G, H, OP-2E, AP-2H, RB-69.

Origin: Lockheed-California.
Type: Maritime reconnaissance bomber.
Engine: Two 3,200 or 3,250hp Wright R-3350-26W or -30W compound radials and two pod-mounted 3,400lb (1540kg) thrust Westinghouse J-34-WE-34 auxiliary turbojets.
Dimensions: (P-2H) span 103ft 10in (31·65m); length 91ft 8in (27·94m); height 29ft 4in (8·94m).
Weight: (P-2H) empty 49,808lb (22,592kg); maximum takeoff weight 79,788lb (36,191kg).
Performance: (P-2H) maximum speed 403mph (648km/h); patrol speed at 1.000ft (305m) 173 to 207mph (278 to 333km/h); range 3,685 miles (5,930km).
Armament: (P-2H) two ·50 caliber machine guns in dorsal turret, sixteen 5in (127mm) rockets; 8,000lb (3629kg) bombs, mines, or depth charges; (P-2E) some models carry two 20mm cannon in a nose turret.
Flight crew: Seven.
History: Two XP2V-1 prototypes ordered in April 1944; more than 1,000 of all types built by 1963; contract for addition of jet auxiliary engines let in October 1954.
Users: US Army (five specially equipped models); US Navy; USAF.

Tactical employment: The Neptune's intended mission was searching for submarines, using magnetic detection gear or acoustic buoys. Besides flying maritime reconnaissance, the plane served as an experimental night attack craft in the attempt to interdict the movement of enemy truck convoys. Another model, the OP-2E, dropped electronic sensors to detect trucks moving along the supply route through southern Laos.

The Neptune received the sensor planting mission because it had precise navigational equipment and accurate optical bombsight. Planners believed that the plane could place the seismic or acoustic device within a few yards of the desired point. To do so, however, the OP-2E had to fly low and level, making it an easy target for the enemy's 37mm guns that were beginning to appear along the trails. Helicopters and eventually F-4 fighters had to take over the task.

Below: Rebuilt nose of an OP-2E of the Navy heading for Laos loaded with ADSID and Spikebuoy sensors in underwing pods.

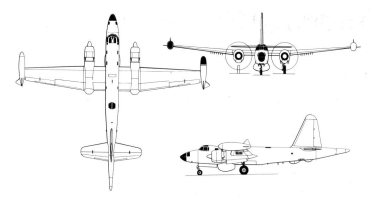

Above: Three-view of basic P-2E, without jet pods.

Above: Another Navy aircraft, a regular P-2H, checks junks offshore. The Air Force and Army used AP-2E and H models.

Lockheed SR-71

SR-71A.

Origin: Lockheed-California.
Type: Two-place strategic reconnaissance craft.
Engines: Two 32,500lb (14,740kg) thrust Pratt & Whitney JT11D-20B (J58) turbojets with afterburners.
Dimensions: Span 55ft 7in (16·95m); length 107ft 5in (32·74m); height 18ft 6in (5·64m)
Weight: Gross weight 107,000lb (48,150kg).
Performance: Maximum speed in excess of 2,000mph (3200km/h); service ceiling over 80,000ft (24,400m); range at least 2,000 miles (3200km) extendable by aerial refueling.
Armament: None.
History: First Flight 22 December 1964; first deliveries of production aircraft January 1966.
User: US Air Force Strategic Air Command.

Below: Longer and heavier than many medium jetliners, the SR-71 is seldom caught at heights that can be reached by ordinary aircraft.

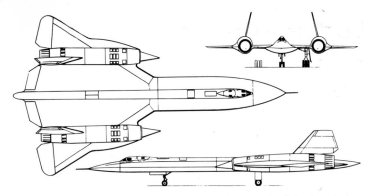

Above: SR-71A three-view; SR-71B and C have raised dual cockpit.

Operational employment: Capable of maintaining surveillance over 60,000 square miles (155,400km²) in just one hour from an altitude of some 80,000 feet (24,400 meters), the SR-71A flew strategic reconnaissance missions over Southeast Asia. Like the older U-2, this aircraft emerged from Kelly Johnson's Lockheed Skunk Works and closely resembled another product of Johnson and his colleagues, the YF-12A.

Described as an interceptor prototype, the YF-12A burst upon the scene in 1964 and during May of the following year established a number of speed records. In the hands of Col. Robert L. Stephens and Lt. Col. Daniel Andre, this near relative of the SR-71A attained a speed of 2,070·102mph (3331·507km/h).

In September of 1974, the SR-71A set some records of its own, thus providing a clue to its performance in the skies over Southeast Asia. Refueling from the KC-135Q, a Boeing Stratotanker especially modified to work with the Blackbird, Majors James B. Sullivan and Noel F. Widdifield flew their SR-71A from New York to London in one hour and 56 minutes. A few days later, Maj. W. C. Machorek and Capt. H. B. Adams flew from London to Los Angeles in three hours, 47 minutes.

Sustained operation at speeds of Mach 3, which was routine in both these long-distance flights, posed severe challenges to Kelly Johnson and his Lockheed team. Temperatures of a thousand degrees fahrenheit, created even in the thin air of the stratosphere, forced the designers to use titanium where they might normally have relied upon aluminum or stainless steel. Speed also raised the specter of compressor stalls as air entered the jet engine intakes at supersonic speed. The engineers solved this problem by installing movable, cone-shaped spikes that extended from the inlets and insured a smooth flow of air.

Below: The unique chined fuselage sections stands out in front view.

Lockheed U-2

U-2A, U-2B, U-2R; data for U-2A.

Origin: Lockheed-California.
Type: Single-place strategic reconnaissance craft.
Engine: One 17,000lb (7711kg) thrust Pratt & Whitney J75-P-13 turbojet.
Dimensions: Span 80ft (24·38m); length 49ft 7in (15·11m); height 13ft (3.9m); U-2R is much larger.
Weight: Gross weight 15,850lb (7190kg).
Performance: Maximum speed 528mph (890km/h); cruising speed 460mph (740km/h); range 4,000 miles (6400km).
Armament: None.
History: Development began 1954; entered service the following year.
User: US Air Force Strategic Air Command.

Tactical employment: Possibly the most important contribution of the U-2 in Southeast Asia was its detection of the first operational surface-to-air missile site in North Vietnam. After taking these pictures in April 1965, this type of plane continued its photographic coverage, gathering information on the evolution of the missile defenses and upon the location of MiG fighters and North Vietnam's handful of Il-28 light bombers.

In brief, the U-2B flew the same sort of high-altitude reconnaissance missions that it had been carrying out since 1955 when, according to legend, one of the earliest models photographed a May Day parade in Moscow, bringing back detailed information on the Russian weapons displayed on that occasion. The plane resulted from the efforts of C. L. "Kelly" Johnson and his colleagues at the Burbank, California, Skunk Works, named after a malodorous factory in the comic strip "Li'l Abner", where Lockheed engineers worked on secret projects. Intended to make unrefueled stratospheric flights lasting as long as eight hours, the U-2 had seemed an impossible dream, for the jet engines of the mid-1950s consumed too much fuel for such an undertaking. Johnson's design team solved this problem by building a powered sail plane with a thin, high-aspect-ratio wing. As a result, the pilot could save fuel and extend his range by shutting down his engine, gliding for a time through the thin air, and then restart the turbojet.

The heart of the U-2B was a camera developed by Edwin Land. From an altitude of 55,000 feet (16,800 meters), this piece of equipment could, it was said, photograph a putting green in such detail that the golf balls were clearly visible.

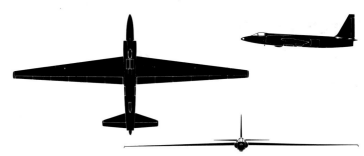

Above: The original U-2A was much smaller than the R variant.

Above: The most important model in Vietnam was the monster U-2R, carrying three times the payload of earlier versions. This R, with wing pods, was seen at U-Tapao RTAFB on 8 April 1975.

Below: Air-to-air of the U-2R, from which today's TR-1 is derived.

Lockheed YO-3

YO-3A, QT-2, Q-Star.

Origin: Lockheed Missile and Space Company.
Type: Two-place special reconnaissance craft.
Engine: (YO-3A) One modified 210hp Continental air-cooled; (Q-Star) 100hp Continental 0-200-A, replaced by a 185hp Wankel rotary combustion type.
Dimensions: (Q-Star, YO-3A) span 57ft (17·37m); length 30ft (9·14m).
Weight: (Q-Star) 2,166lb (983kg).
Performance: Operating speed range (all) 50 to 120kt (58–138mph, 93–222km/h); quietest speed, around 71mph (114km/h); endurance (QT-2) 4hr, (Q-Star, YO-3A) 6hr.
Armament: None.
History: QT-2 first flight 1967, Q-Star first flight 1968, YO-3A prototype contract let July 1968; combat duty (Q-2PC) January 1968, (YO-3A) 1970.
User: US Army.

Tactical employment: By 1966 the US Army had come to realize the value of an airplane that could fly quietly at low altitude, patrolling stealthily and using sensors capable of detecting the Viet Cong and North Vietnamese in spite of darkness. Lockheed engineers attempted to modify a Schweizer two-place glider for this purpose, strengthening the wings, installing a muffled engine, and adding the necessary sensors. Called the QT-2 (standing for quiet thruster, two-place), two prototypes saw action in South Vietnam during February 1968, reportedly flying at an altitude of 100 feet (30 meters) without alerting the enemy.

This success inspired further modifications that resulted in the Lockheed Q-Star. Its airframe further strengthened, this version finally was fitted out

Martin B-57 Canberra

B-57B, G; RB-57E, F.

Origin: The Martin Company.
Type: Light tactical bomber; (RB) multi-sensor reconnaissance.
Engines: Two 7,200lb Wright J-65-W-5 single-shaft turbojets.
Dimensions: Span 64ft (19·51m); length 65ft 6in (19·96m).
Weights: Empty 28,793lb (13,072kg); combat 38,689lb (17,565kg); takeoff 56,965lb (25,862kg).
Performance: Maximum speed at 2,500ft (762m) 520kts; combat radius 824nm (1527m).
Flight crew: Two.
Armament: Four 20mm M-39 guns; 16 rockets; bombload 6,000lb (2724kg).
History: Based on the English Electric Canberra, Britain's first operational jet bomber, built under license in the United States, USAF Tactical Air Command receiving its first B-57 in June 1954.
Users: RAAF; RNZAF; USAF.

Tactical employment: The United States dispatched B-57Bs to South Vietnam in response to the Tonkin Gulf incident in the summer of 1964. On 1 November of that year, Viet Cong demolition teams penetrated the defenses of Bien Hoa to destroy five of the Canberras and damage 15 others. Although vulnerable to ground attack as were all aircraft based in South Vietnam, the B-57B proved itself an effective light bomber, ranging almost to the Cambodian border to attack Viet Cong bases.

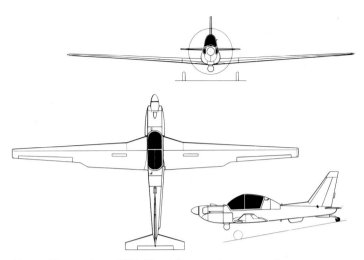

Above: Three-view of YO-3A with ventral sensor pods.

with a Wankel rotary engine, enclosed in a pylon behind the cockpit and attached by means of a long drive shaft to a slowly turning six-blade propeller at the front of the aircraft.

A combat evaluation in South Vietnam produced additional changes that were incorporated in the YO-3A. Instead of the earlier mid-wing design, engineers chose a low-wing arrangement, with a more powerful engine enclosed in the forward fuselage rather than in a dorsal mount. The fixed landing gear gave way to a retractable type, a three-blade propeller was installed, but the principal sensor remained an infrared detector.

Above: USAF B-57G after bomb drop over SE Asia, 6 August 1971.

In March 1965 the United States launched sustained air attacks against North Vietnam, an operation nicknamed Rolling Thunder. This campaign resembled the geographically limited air war against Korea, rather than World War II. The strikes were subject to stringent controls, as the Johnson administration tried to avoid a larger war with China or the Soviet Union. The raids had a threefold purpose: to raise the morale of the South Vietnamese, to punish Hanoi, and to reduce the infiltration of men and supplies in the South. It was also hoped that the operation would bring the North Vietnamese aggressors to the negotiating table. The B-57B figured in the early Rolling Thunder strikes, but vulnerability and difficulty in obtaining spare parts caused it to be shifted to less heavily defended targets.

On 3 April 1965 an Air Force C-130 equipped with flares and accom- ►

Above: A B-57B of the 8th Tactical Bomber Sqn, USAF, based at Phan Ran AB, outward bound on a combat mission in March 1969.

Below: Another B-57B lets go eight 750lb bombs (four internal, four external) on a Vietnam target in December 1967.

▶ panied by two B-57s flew a night mission over routes 12, 23, and 121 in the southern panhandle of Laos. The crews searched for communist vehicles and other enemy targets moving down the Ho Chi Minh Trail towards South Vietnam and Cambodia. The mission marked the beginning of Operation Steel Tiger, an interdiction campaign against enemy troop and supply movements. Although no longer able to brave the improving defense in North Vietnam, the B-57 performed effectively in Laos, especially when modified for armed reconnaissance at night. The B models departed Southeast Asia in 1969, leaving behind the squadron of Gs.

The B-57G could find the enemy at night and attack him. Faced with serious problems regarding night strike operations, the US Air Force had tried out several aircraft for the task, including the B-26, C-123, and the A-1. In March 1967 it decided to equip three B-57B aircraft with an infrared sensor. The aircraft with the modification known as Tropic Moon II arrived at Phan Rang, South Vietnam, on 12 December. Another infrared modification program begun in 1967 on the B-57G became known as Tropic Moon III. This project involved considerable equipment at great cost and eventually included new weapons, computers and navigational system, additional armor plating, ejection seats, and self-sealing tanks. During 1968 a total of 16 B-57Gs underwent modification. Numerous mechanical problems beset the project and it dragged on unfinished for many months. But once the work was accomplished, the G models served as night intruders until the spring of 1972.

The B-57s were the first jet aircraft turned over to the South Vietnamese Air Force. On 9 August 1965 the first of four B-57s was turned over. By the end of the year four VNAF crews began flying training missions with the Air Force B-57 unit stationed at Da Nang. The plane, however, did not become a permanent element of South Vietnam's Air Force.

Crews from Australia and New Zealand flew British-built Canberras during the war. These were plexiglass-nosed versions used for medium altitude bombing using an optical sight. These planes saw action exclusively in South Vietnam.

Reconnaissance variants of the B-57 flew missions in Southeast Asia employing cameras and infrared sensors. Use of the latter device, which proved valuable against an enemy who moved by night, was pioneered by the RB-57E

Above: B-57Bs often flew night FAC missions with various target markers, but this one is carrying M116/A1 thick-fuel fire bombs.

Below: Canberra B.20 of No 2 Sqn, RAAF, outward bound on attack mission from Phan Rang AB on 23 March 1970.

Martin P-5 Marlin

SP-5B.

Origin: The Martin Company.
Type: Antisubmarine warfare flying boat.
Engines: Two 3,450hp Wright R-3350-32WA Turbo-Compound radials.
Dimensions: Span 118ft 2½in (36·0m); length 100ft 7¼in (30·66m); height 32ft 8½in (9·97m).
Weight: Empty 50,485lb (22,900kg); loaded 76,635lb (34,761kg).
Performance: Maximum speed at sea level 251mph (404km/h); patrol range 2,050 miles (3300km); ferry range 3,100 miles (4,990km).
Armament: Up to 8,000lb (3,629kg) of bombs, torpedoes, or mines.
Flight crew: Eleven.
History: First flight August 1953; first delivery to US Navy 23 June 1954; production ended 20 December 1960.
User: US Navy.

Tactical employment: The P-5B, originally P5M-2, was an improved version of the first twin-engine flying boat built for the postwar US Navy to locate and attack submarines. Besides radar, the Marlin carried magnetic airborne detection gear, which could discover a submerged U-boat. The Marlin patrolled the Tonkin Gulf until 1965.

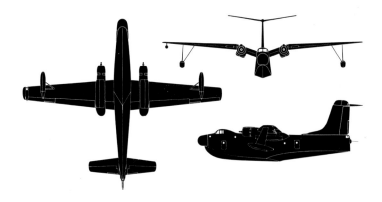

Above: Three-view of basic P-5B without additional electronics.

Right: An SP-5B at dusk on 15 March 1966 as it circled over Cam Ranh Bay.

Left: View from the cockpit of an SP-5B taxiing across Cam Ranh Bay on 13 March 1966 having just left the parent tender, USS *Salisbury Sound*, seen in the background with another Marlin hoisted on board (note crane).

Below: One of the last SP-5B Marlins, pictured on 7 May 1967 with VP-40, the last flying boat unit in the theatre.

McDonnell Douglas A-4 Skyhawk

A-4C, D, E, TA-4E, A-4F, A-4M.

Origin: Douglas Aircraft Co., El Segundo (division of McDonnell Douglas Long Beach).

Type: Single-seat carrier-based attack bomber; (TA-4C, F dual-control trainers).

Engines: (C) one 7,700lb (3493kg) thrust Wright J65-16A single-shaft turbojet; (E) 8,500lb (3856kg) Pratt & Whitney J52-6 two-shaft turbojet.

Dimensions: Span 27ft 6in (8·38m); length 40ft 3¼in (12·27m); height 15ft (4·51m).

Weights: Empty (A) 7,700lb (3500kg); (E) 9,284lb (4220kg); (TA-4F) 10,602lb (4809kg); max takeoff all others (shipboard) except (A) 24,500lb (11,113kg); (land-based) 27,420lb (12,437kg).

Performance: Maximum speed (E) 675mph (1086km/h).

Armament: Standard on most versions two 20mm MK 12 cannon, each with 200 rounds; two 30mm DEFA 553 each with 150 rounds. Pylons under fuselage and wings for total ordnance load of (A, B, C) 5,000lb (2268kg), (E, F) 8,200lb (3720kg).

History: First flight (A-4C) August 1959; (A-4E) July 1961; (A-4F) August 1966; (TA-4E) June 1965.

Users: US Navy, US Marine Corps, and US Air Force.

Above: Popularly called "The Scooter" by its pilots, the A-4 was a troublefree aircraft on a carrier; this is a catapult launch.

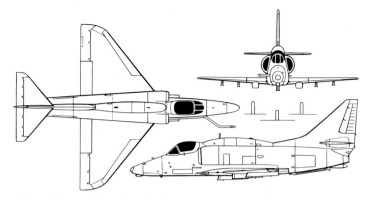

Above: Three-view of A-4M Skyhawk II (with Camel hump).

Tactical employment: Douglas Aircraft intended to provide the Navy and Marine Corps with an inexpensive, lightweight attack and ground support aircraft. The design emphasized low-speed control and stability during ▶

Left: A-4C Skyhawk of VA-144, aboard USS *Kittyhawk*, Danang.

Below: These Sky-hawks are almost certainly of the A-4E model, without dorsal avionic hump but with inflight-refuelling probe. These were en route to a Vietnam target from the carrier *Oriskany* in the first quarter of 1965.

►take-off and landing as well as strength enough for catapult launch and carrier landings. The plane was so compact that it did not need folding wings for aboardship storage and handling.

The A-4 first saw action in Vietnam in the summer of 1964 when the carriers of Task Force 77 retaliated for attacks by North Vietnamese torpedo boats on one American destroyer and repeated attacks on another. Skyhawks joined other aircraft in the raiding of PT bases at Loc Chou. The A-4 then became involved in a 37 month bombing effort of North Vietnam (Rolling Thunder), beginning on 7 February 1965.

During Rolling Thunder, two A-4Es became the first Navy aircraft shot down by surface-to-air missiles. On the night of 13/14 August 1965, the two planes were flying a reconnaissance mission south of Hanoi when the pilots noticed two flares, glowing beneath the clouds and coming closer. The pilots realized too late that burning missile propellant was the source of the light. One A-4 exploded and crashed, while the other limped back to the carrier *Midway* with a horribly scorched and peppered belly.

In April 1966 as Rolling Thunder continued, 11 A-4s from the carrier *Ticonderoga* participated in a strike against the Haiphong highway bridge, one of the largest bridges leading into that city from Red China. Drop tanks were removed from the aircraft as the Navy reasoned that weather conditions would allow a successful small "clean wing" maximum load attack. Despite heavy flak and several SAM assaults the mission was successful. Five of the 21 bridge spans were knocked out and the group returned to base with only slight damage to one A-4 and the loss of an escorting F-8.

Marine Skyhawks, flown in from bases in Japan and Hawaii, also took part in thwarting the North Vietnamese spring invasion of 1972. In spite of its diminutive size, the A-4 packed a devastating punch. Its two-place versions, originally intended as trainers, saved the Marines' forward air controllers over heavily defended areas where speed and maneuverability were essential for survival.

Left: These Skyhawks are relatively early A-4C models, from the Carrier Air Group embarked aboard USS *Constellation*. Note steam issuing from the catapult being readied for next shot.

Below left: Skyhawks from two Navy attack squadrons, VA-55 and VA-164, ranged aboard one of the smaller carriers, USS *Hancock*.

Below: An A-4E Skyhawk fires a salvo of three-inch unguided rockets against a VC concentration. Like most of the greatest combat aircraft the A-4 was continually being updated, this version having a new engine and increased 8,200lb (3720kg) bombload.

McDonnell Douglas F-4 Phantom II

F-4B, C, E, RF-4B, C.

Origin: McDonnell Aircraft, division of McDonnell Douglas Corp.
Type: Two-place, twin-engine, long-range. all-weather attack fighter or reconnaissance craft.
Engines: (B, C, D) two 17,000lb (7711kg) General Electric J79-GE-8 or -15 afterburning turbojets; (E) two J79-GE-17s, 17,000lb st (8120kg).
Dimensions: Span 38ft 5in (11·70m); length (B, C, D) 58ft 3in (17·76m); (E and all RF versions) 62ft 11in or 63ft (19·2m).
Weights: Empty (B, C, D) 28,000lb (12,700kg); (E, RF) 29,000lb (13,150kg); maximum loaded (B) 54,000lb (24,818kg); (C, D, RF) 58,000lb (26,380kg); (E) 60,630lb (27,502kg).
Performance: Max level speed without external stores over Mach 2; approach speed 150mph (240km/h); takeoff run (interceptor) 5,000ft (1525m); landing run (interceptor) 3,000ft (915m); combat radius (interceptor) over 900 miles (1450km), (ground attack) over 994 miles (1600km); ferry range 2,300 miles (3700km).
Armament: Six Sparrow III, or four Sparrow III and four Sidewinder air-to-air missiles on four semi-submerged mountings under fuselage and two underwing mountings. (E) versions except RF have internal 20mm M61 multi-barrel gun, and most versions carry the same gun in external centreline pod. Typical loads include eighteen 750lb (340kg) bombs, eleven 150 US gallon napalm bombs, four Bullpup air-to-surface missiles or 15 air-to-surface missiles or 15 air-to-surface rockets.
Flight crew: 2.

Right: Despite its relatively comprehensive navigation systems the F-4 was not equipped for accurate level bomb delivery from medium altitudes. The technique perfected in Vietnam was to bomb on signal from a fully equipped lead-ship, in this case an RB-66C (also see p 57).

Below: Individual bombing by an F-4B of VF-21, USS _Midway_.

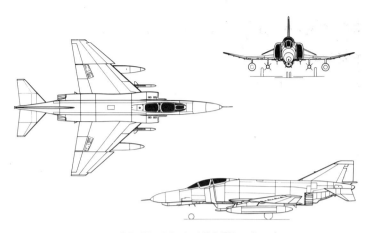

Above: Three-view of F-4E with six AIM-7E and tanks.

History: First Flight of F-4C 27 May 63; F-4C entered operational service 20 November 1963; RF-4C first flight (production aircraft) 18 May 1964, entered operational service 24 September 1964; F-4D first flight (production aircraft) 8 December 1965; F-4E first flight 30 June 1967, entered operational service 3 October 1967.

Users: US Air Force (F-4C, E, RF-4C), Navy and Marine Corps (F-4B, E).

Tactical employment: The F-4 was used extensively in Vietnam. The F-4B, for example, served the Marines as a fighter-bomber and interceptor, and the Navy as an all-weather fighter. The Air Force, which had adopted the F-4C in 1962, despatched the plane to Southeast Asia in early 1965, ▶

Below: An F-4B rolls into its final firing pass with the last pair of rocket pods in April 1966. It has a single Sparrow AAM.

Above: F-4B from VMFA (Marine Aircraft Group 11, 1st MAW) outward bound from Da Nang on ground support.

▶ and Phantoms scored their first MiG-17 kills on 10 July 1965. By March 1966 seven F-4C squadrons were engaged in combat. In two years of aerial fighting 1965 and 1966, 54 F-4Cs were lost in combat.

The Air Force believed that a cannon was better suited than air-to-air rockets for combat against the MiG, so a pod-mounted M-61A1 20mm gun was installed. Some F-4Cs were modified for the Air Force's Wild Weasel program. These versions carried ECM warning sensors, vectoring equipment, jamming pods, chaff dispensers and anti-radiation missiles.

The RF-4C, similar to the F-4C, was modified for photographic and electronic reconnaissance missions. In Southeast Asia, this aircraft supplanted the RF-101 as the standard Air Force tactical reconnaissance plane. The principal drawback of the RF-4C was the need for illumination for night photography. Photo flash cartridges, ejected from the plane's fuselage gave the necessary light but also alerted enemy gunners. The naval equivalent of this model was the RF-4B.

The F-4D arrived in Southeast Asia in May 1967 and was stationed at Ubon with the 555th TFS. The D models were improved with the installation of a lead-computing sight and a central air data computer for both bombing and navigation. The computer automatically determined the weapon release point for all bombing modes—dive or level, at night or in bad

Below: Fully bomb-laden F-4B of VF-84 embarked aboard USS _Independence_ in 1968. Note Jolly Roger unit insignia.

weather. This version of the Phantom II launched Walleye television-guided missiles and laser-guided bombs. The F-4D gradually replaced the C types, even taking over the Wild Weasel mission.

The F-4E was similar to the F-4D with the exception of an improved later model engine and improved tactical capabilities. They were also fitted with Skyspot radar (which helped radar operators on the ground track the planes), beacons, and with more effective electronic countermeasures pods.

The F-4 ranked behind the F-105 in Southeast Asia combat losses—362, the majority of which were combat-related. The Phantom II played an important role in the reinforcement of South Vietnam after the North Vietnamese invasion at Easter 1972. Stationed in Thailand some 76 F-4s flew both day and night missions pounding North Vietnamese targets. During the course of the war F-4C, D and Es accounted for 107 MiG kills.

Below: Vortices streaming, an Air Force F-4C pulls g carrying napalm. Such operations resulted in the slatted F-4E variant, the slatted wing being introduced with this model.

Below: Return from combat (note carrier); some of this F-4B's AIM-7 and AIM-9 air/air missiles have been fired.

McDonnell RF-101 Voodoo

RF-101C.

Origin: McPonnell Aircraft.
Type: Single-seat tactical reconnaissance craft.
Engine: Two 14,500lb (6575kg) thrust Pratt & Whitney J57-P-13 afterburning turbojets.
Dimensions: Span 39ft 8in (12·09m); length 69ft (21·04m); height 18ft (5·49m).
Weight: Maximum takeoff weight 48,100lb (21,818·02kg).
Performance: Maximum speed 1,000mph (1609·8km/h); cruising speed 552mph (885·9km/h); ferry range 2,145 miles (3452·9km).
Armament: None.
History: Based on F-101A interceptor; first flight 12 July 1957; first production aircraft accepted September 1957; production ended March 1959.
User: US Air Force Tactical Air Command, PACAF.

Tactical employment: The RF-101 first saw action in Southeast Asia during October 1961, taking off from Tan Son Nhut air base near Saigon to fly photo missions over the Ho Chi Minh Trail, the principal communist supply line through southern Laos, and the Plain of Jars to the northwest, where Russian Il-14P transports were delivering supplies to communist and neutralist troops. After these Voodoos departed, others arrived at Don Muang airfield in Thailand and began conducting reconnaissance over South Vietnam and Laos. Late in 1962, after the establishment of a coalition government in Laos, aerial reconnaissance of the kingdom ended, only to resume in 1964 with the approval of Prince Souvanna Phouma, the prime minister, who was concerned about clashes between communist and non-communist factions.

At the time of this early service in Southeast Asia, the RF-101C was undergoing extensive structural repair. Stress fractures had appeared in several places, including the metal skin of the wing and fuselage and on the main wing spar. An inspection and repair facility on Okinawa performed the necessary work on those planes assigned to Pacific Air Forces.

On 8 February 1965, RF-101Cs accompanied the first US Air Force strike against North Vietnam. Instead of taking pictures, however, the Voodoos navigated for an attack force made up of F-100Ds. The career as pathfinder proved brief, and the planes reverted to their normal photographic mission. On one such flight near Yen Bay, two MiG-17s pounced on a pair of Voodoos; one of the reconnaissance pilots continued his run, while the other offered himself as a decoy, drew the attention of the MiGs, and outran

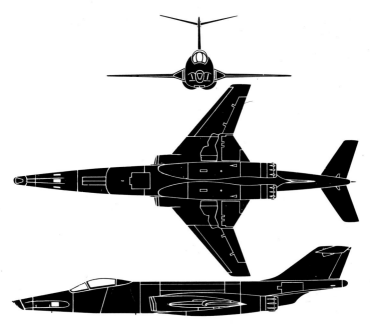

Above: Three-view of RF-101C (later backed up by G and H).

them, allowing the other to complete its mission.

Although fast enough to leave a MiG-17 far behind, the RF-101C could not race away from faster MiG-21s. In September 1967, during surveillance of North Vietnamese airfields, one of the later-model MiGs shot down a Voodoo. Seventh Air Force headquarters decided to ban this reconnaissance craft from the skies over North Vietnam and rely on the McDonnell Douglas RF-4C, with its greater speed, its more modern cameras, and its infrared sensor and side-looking airborne radar. By the end of the year, only the Phantom II conducted low-to-medium-altitude photo missions for the US Air Force over North Vietnam.

Gradually, the RF-4C replaced the RF-101C altogether. The first Voodoo squadron supplanted by the Phantom II disbanded in October 1967; the last left Tan Son Nhut in August 1971, almost nine years after the type had flown its first missions over Laos. Meanwhile, the Air Force had begun transferring the RF-101C to the Air National Guard, a process completed during 1971.

Left: Recovery at Udorn RTAFB of an RF-101C after a combat sortie. An outstanding reconnaissance platform, it looked 'hot' yet established an exceptional record of safe operation.

Mikoyan-Gurevich MiG-17

MiG-17 and 17F (Chinese F-4, NATO name "Fresco").

Origin: Design bureau of Mikoyan and Gurevich, Soviet Union.
Type: Single-seat fighter, limited all weather interceptor.
Engine: (C) One 7,590lb (3450kg) thrust Kilmov VK-1A turbojet engine.
Dimensions: Span 36ft (10·96m); length 40ft (12·20m); height 11ft (3·35m).
Weights: Empty 9,850lb (4470kg); normal takeoff weight 13,200lb (5990kg); maximum takeoff weight 15,000lb (7030kg).
Performance: Maximum speed Mach 0·975; landing speed 127mph (211km/h); rate of climb 10,500ft/min (3200m/min); service ceiling 57,100ft (17,400m), normal range 510 miles (820km); range with external tanks 1,160 miles (1860km).
Armament: Usually, three 23mm Nudelmann-Rikter NR-23 cannon. Provision for two underwing packs of 8×55mm air-to-air rockets or a total of 1,100lb (500kg) of bombs.
History: First flight (prototype) January 1950; service delivery, 1952; final delivery 1959.
User: North Vietnam.
Tactical employment: The MiG-17 (Fresco) was an advanced version of the MiG-15. The earliest F-4 variants served basically as day fighters in Vietnam, while later versions also performed as fighter-bombers or limited all-weather and night fighters. Although never considered the deadliest North Vietnamese fighter, the MiG-17 was heavily armed and highly maneuverable, especially at low altitudes where it could turn inside heavier American jets and use its 23mm weapons to good effect. Nevertheless, USAF accounts list 61 MiG-17s downed in dogfights.

Because of stepped-up attacks against targets in North Vietnam, Hanoi ordered its MiGs into action to supplement the antiaircraft defences. On 23 April 1966 two flights of MiG-17s under GCI control attempted to intercept some F-105s returning from their targets. Anticipating a confrontation with the F-105s the MiG-17s were surprised by a pack of F-4s flying MiG Screen in support of the Thunderchiefs, and in the ensuing moments two MiG-17s were downed.

In May 1966, Major Wilbur R. Dudley and First Lieutenant Imats Kringelis, F-4 pilots of the 555th Tactical Fighter Squadron, were escorting an EB-66 on an electronic warfare mission over the Red River Valley when jumped by four MiG-17s nearly 110 miles northwest of Hanoi. According to Major Dudley, one MiG-17 pilot made the grievous mistake of concentrating on the EB-66 and ignoring the fighter escort.

Dudley approached the MiG from behind, missed with his first Sidewinder shot, but fired again when the North Vietnamese pilot rolled out

Below: A MiG-17F of the North Vietnamese Air Force.

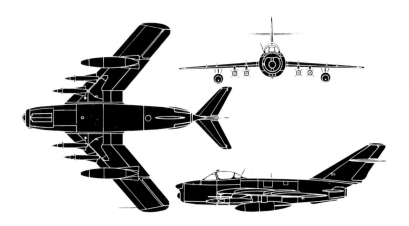

Above: Three-view of gunless MiG-17PFU with Alkali AAMs.

behind the EB-66. This time his heat-seeking missile guided up the MiG's tailpipe and the aircraft disintegrated. This mission caused a controversy, when Chinese officials charged that Dudley had shot down his victim over Yunan Province, some 25 miles north of the North Vietnamese border. ▶

Left: An exceptional combat photograph of a MiG-17F taken early in the Vietnam war prior to 1967. In general a well-flown MiG-17, like the MiG-21, could outmaneuver any of the US fighters, despite its obsolete design concept.

Mikoyan/Gurevich MiG-19

MiG-19S, -19SF (Chinese F-6)

Origin: The design bureau of Mikoyan and Gurevich, Soviet Union.
Type: Single-seat fighter/bomber.
Engines: Two 7,165lb (3250kg) thrust (afterburner rating) Tumanskii RD-9B single-shaft afterburning turbojets.
Dimensions: Span 36ft 6in (11·1m); length 44ft 3in (13·49m); height 13ft 6in (4·10m).
Weight: Maximum takeoff weight 19,840lb (9000kg).
Performance: Maximum speed at 20,000ft (6000m) Mach 1·3; normal range 600 miles (965km), maximum range with external tanks 850 miles (1370km).
Armament: All F-6 models in Vietnam, two or three 30mm NR-30 cannon. Also the aircraft has the ability to carry air-to-air missiles or four underwing pods, each containing 8×55mm rockets.
History: First flight September 1953; service delivery early 1955.
User: North Vietnam.

Tactical employment: In the Vietnam War the MiG-19 performed as a day fighter, interceptor, and night or all-weather fighter. The MiG-19 had generally better performance than the MiG-17, but lacked some of the latter's "cut-and-thrust" maneuverability. The newer aircraft appeared in Vietnam only after the 1968 bombing halt. Apparently the Chinese both supplied the aircraft and trained the North Vietnamese pilots. The MiG-19 lacked the speed and maneuverability of the MiG-21 and was thus easier to defeat in a dogfight. Since it saw infrequent combat in Vietnam, only ten were destroyed during the war, eight by the US Air Force and two by the Navy.

USAF pilots scored more victories over the MiG-19 on MiGCAP (Combat Air Patrols directed specifically against MiG aircraft) flights than any other means. On 12 May 1972, in a typical encounter Colonel Wayne T. Frye,

Mikoyan/Gurevich MiG-21

MiG-21F, -21PF, -21PFM (Chinese F-7)

Manufacturer: Soviet Union design bureau named for Mikoyan and Gurevich, designers of the initial MiG series.
Type: Single-seat multi-role fighter.
Engine: In all versions of the MiG-21, one Tumansky single-shaft turbojet with afterburner; (early models) R-11 rated at 11,240lb (5100kg) with afterburner; (later) 14,550lb (6600kg) R-13-300.
Dimensions: Span 23ft 5½in (7·15m); length (excluding probe) 46ft 11in; height 14ft 9in (4·5m).
Weight: Empty (MiG-21) 11,464lb (5200kg); maximum loaded 18,740lb (8500kg).
Performance: Maximum level speed above 36,000ft (11,000m) 1,385mph (Mach 2·1, 2230km/h); maximum level speed at low altitude 807mph (Mach 1·06, 1300km/h). *continued▶*

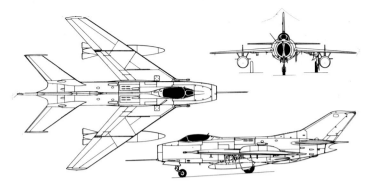

Above: Three-view of MiG-19SF (F-6).

Left: MiG-19SF of North Vietnam Air Force. Notable features of this aircraft were its superb finish, outstanding dogfight manouverability and the tremendous hitting power of its NR-30 guns.

Commander of the 555th Tactical Fighter Squadron and Colonel James P. Cooney brought down the unit's first MiG-19. Their F-4s encountered the victim at low altitude (500 to 1,000ft, 152 to 304m), about 2 miles (3·2km) southwest of Yen Bai airfield. They fired three AIM-7s at one MiG-19 in a flight of four and dived past the enemy formation. Colonel Frye looked back and spotted a cloud of debris where the MiG-19 had been.

On 23 May that same year two MiG-19s were spotted south of Kep air-field in North Vietnam by an F-4 pilot, Lt Colonel Lyle L. Beckers, who was about seven miles distant. He began the chase at 500 knots and eased down on the aircraft, and with the help of cloud cover was able to get within 2,000ft (610m) without detection. After descending to 2,000ft to get a good look-up angle for the radar he fired two AIM-7s; the first scored a direct hit, and the other came within 20 feet (6m) but failed to detonate.

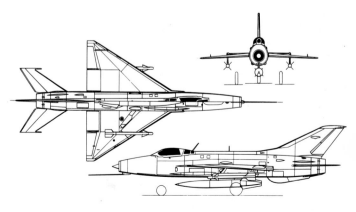

Above: Three-view of MiG-21F (Fishbed C).

▶ Armament: One twin barrel 23mm GSh-23 gun, with 200 rounds in belly pack. Four underwing pylons for weapons or drop tanks. Typical load for interceptor includes two K-13A (Atoll) air-to-air missiles on inner pylons and two radar-homing Advanced Atolls or two UV-16-57 (rocket packs each sixteen 57mm rockets) on outer pylons.

Flight crew: One.

History: First flight (E-5 prototype) late-1955; (pre-production) late 1957; service delivery early 1958.

User: North Vietnam.

Tactical employment: The MiG-21 was developed as an air superiority fighter on the basis of experience of air-to-air combat between MiG-17s and US aircraft during the Korean War. First versions of the MiG-21 were day fighters with limited range, light armament and limited avionics. In later versions the range, weapons and all-weather capabilities were improved. In Vietnam the MiG-21 proved capable of challenging all but the most modern US fighters. Its many versions played such roles as all-weather interceptor, day point-defense interceptor and clear-weather fighter.

The North Vietnamese MiG-21s had their problems with US fighters. Indeed, American airmen received credit for shooting down some 68 MiG-21s during the course of the war. The first MiG-21 was shot down on 26 April 1966 by an F-4C flying combat air patrol. After this fight, MiG formations seemed reluctant to engage large numbers of F-4Cs. Indeed, the MiG-21 was used mostly for high-altitude interception, possibly because North Vietnamese pilots were just gaining experience with it.

In August 1967 the North Vietnamese began using MiG-21s in hit-and-run attacks on American fighter-bombers. Flying in pairs at low level, keeping within radar ground clutter until they were close astern of an inbound strike formation, the MiG-21 pilots would ignite their afterburners and climb above the US force. Then, using GCI radar vectoring, they would make shallow passes at speeds in excess of Mach 1, fire their missiles, and either climb steeply or continue through the US formation. After one firing pass, the MiGs would break contact and scatter, sometimes seeking refuge in China. This tactic proved effective—from August 1967 through the end of February 1968 MiG-21s lost just five of their number while downing 18 American fighters.

By early 1972 the North Vietnamese had 93 MiG-21s available for action. The Americans more than held their own, shooting down 24 of the Soviet-built fighters from February through July, at a cost of 18 planes. During the B-52 attacks upon North Vietnam in December 1972, MiG-21s shadowed the night bombers, determining the proper detonating altitude for surface-to-air missiles. One of the fighters ventured too close to one of the bombers and fell victim to the tail gunner's 50-caliber fire.

Above: A North Vietnamese Air Force MiG-21PFMA.

Left: Few good photographs exist of aircraft of the VPAF (Vietnam People's Air Air Force). Though a much larger number was supplied, it never had more than about 90 MiG-21s serviceable, most of them of the MiG-21PF type as seen here. Pilots mainly had extremely limited flying experience.

North American F-100 Super Sabre

F-100C, D, F.

Origin: North American Aviation, Inc.
Type: Single-place (C, D), two-seat (F) fighter bomber.
Engine: (D, F) 16,950lb (7690kg) J57-21A (with afterburner).
Dimensions: Span (D, F) 38ft 9½in (11·81m); length (D) 49ft 6in (15·09m), (F) 52ft 6in (16·0m); height (D, F) 16ft 2¾in (4·96m).
Weights: Empty (D) 21,000lb (9525kg); (F) 22,300lb (10,115kg); maximum loaded (D) 34,832lb (15,800kg); (F, two tanks but no weapons), 30,700lb (13,925kg).
Performance: Maximum speed (D, F) 864mph at height (1390km/h, Mach 1·31); initial climb (clear) 16,000ft/min (4900m/min); service ceiling (typical) 45,000ft (13,720m); range (high, two 375gal tanks) 1,500 miles (2415km).
Armament: Usually, (D) four or (F) two 20mm M-39E cannon each with 200 rounds; (D) two tanks and six pylons for 7,500lb (3402kg) ordnance; (F) two tanks and maximum of 6,000lb (2722kg) ordnance.
History: (D) first flight (production aircraft) 24 January 1956; first acceptance (production aircraft) April 1956; entered operational service 29 September 1956; (F) first flight (production aircraft) 7 March 1957; first acceptance January 1958.
User: US Air Force Tactical Air Command, PACAF.

Tactical employment: The F-100 first saw action in Southeast Asia in May of 1962 when several were sent to Thailand from the 13th Air Force in response to communist incursions into northwest Laos.

F-100 operations in Vietnam began in 1965 and on 8 February that year F-100s took part in Operation Flaming Dart, the first US Air Force strike against North Vietnam, and in the subsequent Rolling Thunder attacks. Further deployments of the aircraft to the area left just five F-100D squadrons in the United States.

Below: Unlike most other Western combat types the 'Hun' was good at top cover and low attack; here an F-100D begins a strafing run.

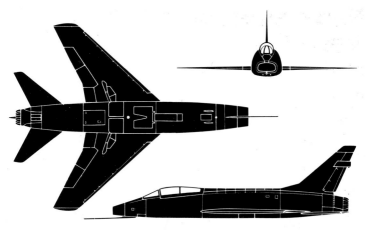

Above: Three-view of F-100D in unusual clean condition.

Above: This F-100D is seen with supersonic finned tanks, four bombs and flight-refuelling probe. It may have logged 4,000 hours.

Because of the F-100's ability to carry a heavy load of munitions, which it exhibited in Vietnam, the Air Force examined the aircraft's wings for signs of corrosion, which could be corrected to prolong the plane's life-span. The Air Force and the prime contractor also examined the lower wing skin in order to redesign it for further use. Finally, in late 1967 the Air Force developed a complete structural modification plan for the wing and, by 1969, center wing sections of 682 F-100Ds had been modified.

Other modifications enhanced the combat effectiveness of the F-100. Modifications included a Motorola SST-181 X-band radar transmitter, which provided a ground directed bombing capability for night and bad weather missions. In addition, the weapon release and firing systems were improved and new guns and a more accurate target-marking system were added.

Earlier modifications had been completed on seven two-place F-100Fs designated "Wild Weasel I". These aircraft had the APR-25 vector radar homing and warning (RHAW) receiver to detect S-band signals (emitted by by SA-2 fire control radar and early warning/ground controlled intercept radar), and C-band signals (from improved SA-2) and the X-band airborne intercept radar. Four aircraft were deployed to Korat, Thailand, on 21 November 1965 and assigned to the 388th Tactical Fighter Wing, and the following month began to fly war missions. Three more Wild Weasel I air-▶

►craft were deployed to the Southeast Asia theater in February 1966 to participate in "Iron Hand" anti-SAM air campaign. In 1966 some Wild Weasel F-100Fs began using AGM-45 Shrike missiles, designed to home on radar transmitters, a weapon introduced by naval aviators flying the A-4C. Thanks to the Shrike, F-100Fs could attack the North Vietnamese missile control radars from a comparatively safe distance.

Above: A pair of F-100D single-seaters parked between missions. F-100s flew more missions in Vietnam than 15,586 P-51s in WW2.

Below: F-100D-6 (56-2910) of 308th Tactical Fighter Sqdn, 31st TFW, Tuy Hoa, Vietnam, 1970.

The only F-100Cs to serve in South Vietnam arrived in the spring of 1968 and remained about a year. The aircraft belonged to US Air National Guard squadrons mobilized as a result of North Korea's capture of the American intelligence ship *Pueblo*. Air Force planners decided that the elderly C models could perform a greater service in the more permissive skies of South Vietnam than over the Korean peninsula.

North American RA-5 Vigilante

RA-5C.

Origin: North American Aviation.
Type: Two-seat reconnaissance plane.
Engines: Two 17,000lb (7711kg) thrust General Electric J79-GE-8 afterburning turbojets.
Dimensions: Span 53ft (16·15m); length 75ft 10in (23·11m); height 19ft 4¾in (5·91m).
Weight: Maximum takeoff weight about 80,000lb (36,285kg).
Performance: Maximum level speed Mach 2·1 — 1,385mph (2230km/h) — at 40,000ft (12,190m); long-range cruising speed 560mph (900km/h) at 40,000ft (12,190m); normal range 2,650 miles (4260km).
Armament: None as reconnaissance craft.
History: First flight of reconnaissance version 30 June 1962; based on an attack plane (XA3J-1), built to deliver nuclear weapons, first flown 31 August 1958.
User: US Navy.

Tactical employment: The first Vigilantes that joined the fleet in 1961 were attack planes, capable of attaining twice the speed of sound. Their bomb bays could accommodate a nuclear weapon to which a pair of auxiliary fuel tanks had been attached. The twin turbojet engines burned this fuel en route to the target so that the bomb and the empty tanks could be ejected together from the rear of the tunnel shaped weapons bay. The fuel containers improved the bomb's aerodynamic traits as it plummeted toward earth. The second model, the A-5B was also intended as an attack plane; it carried additional internal fuel in tanks behind the cockpit.

   The RA-5C reconnaissance craft, which closely resembled the B model, retained the weapons bay and extra internal fuel capacity found in the attack version. The sensors mounted in the RA-5C included vertical and oblique cameras, infrared equipment, and side-looking airborne radar.

One of the most successful uses of the T-28 was on hunter-killer missions teamed with an O-1F that mounted a starlight scope. On these missions a forward air controller in the 0-1 would take off thirty minutes before the T-28 and position himself, following instructions from a radar site on the ground, along a stretch of road. The O-1F waited, using shielded navigation lights, which could only be viewed from above, to mark its position for the T-28.

Circling 1,000ft (309m) above the O-1F, the T-28 pilot waited for the forward air controller to detect trucks with his scope, then dived to the attack according to the controller's instructions. The T-28 could also perform the same mission with any aircraft equipped with a night vision scope, such as the C-123 or C-130.

Long after they had proved too vulnerable to survive the increasingly accurate antiaircraft fire over southern Laos, T-28s, sometimes flown by Thai volunteers, saw action in the northern part of that kingdom. For most of the war, the T-28D served as the principal attack plane of the Royal Lao Air Force.

Left: In the 1960s North American extensively rebuilt 321 T-28As as T-28D Co-In armed attack aircraft, Fairchild Hiller converting 72 more. The 800hp R-1300 engine of the trainer was replaced by an R-1820 and stores pylons added.

North American OV-10 Bronco

OV-10A.

Origin: North American Rockwell.
Type: Two-seat counterinsurgency aircraft.
Engine: Two 715hp AiResearch T76-G-10, -12 turboprops.
Dimensions: Span 40ft (12·19m); length 41ft 7in (12·67m); height 15ft 2in (4·62m).
Weight: Empty 6,969lb (3161kg); normal takeoff weight 9,908lb (4494kg).
Performance: Maximum speed at sea level without armament 281mph (452km/h); combat radius with maximum weapons load 228 miles (367km/h).
Armament: Four attachment points on sponsons extending from either side of the fuselage, each accommodating 600lb (272kg); a fifth attachment point, under the crew pod, capable of carrying 1,200lb (544kg); two 0·30-caliber machine guns in each sponson. Maximum weapons load 3,600lb (1633kg).
History: First flight by prototype YOV-10A 16 July 1965; first production orders by Marine Corps and Air Force October 1966; first flight by production model 6 August 1967.
Users: US Air Force Tactical Air Command, PACAF, US Marine Corps.

Tactical employment: Among the aircraft most feared by the Viet Cong and North Vietnamese forces was the OV-10A, for whenever the Bronco appeared overhead, an air strike seemed certain to follow. Although the glassed-in cabin could become uncomfortably warm, it provided splendid visibility. The two-man crew enjoyed armor protection and could use machine guns and bombs to attack, as well as rockets to mark targets for fighter-bombers. This versatility enabled the plane to fly armed reconnaissance missions, in addition to serving as vehicle for forward air controllers. The Bronco could carry a laser device to pinpoint targets at night for fighters carrying laser-guided bombs.

Right: The superb view from the OV-10A is evident from the gold-fish-bowl effect of this photograph taken by a backseater.

Below: While some Marine Corps OV-10As were non-standard black overall, the USAF Broncos were light grey with small markings.

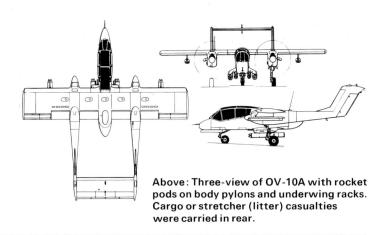

Above: Three-view of OV-10A with rocket pods on body pylons and underwing racks. Cargo or stretcher (litter) casualties were carried in rear.

Northrop F-5 Freedom Fighter

F-5A, B, E.

Origin: Northrop Corporation, Aircraft Division.

Type: A single-seat supersonic fighter designed for close air support, air defense and interdiction mission. The F-5B is a two-seat version designed for fighter/trainer duties. The F-5E is a single-seat air superiority fighter.

Engines: Two General Electric J85-GE-13 afterburning turbojets each with maximum rating of 4,080lb (1850kg) st.

Dimensions: Span (no tip tanks) 25ft 3in (7·07m); length (A) 47ft 2in (14·38m), (B) 46ft 4in (14·12m); height (A) 13ft 2in (4·01m).

Weights: Empty, equipped (A) 8,085lb (3667kg), (B) 8,361lb (3792kg); loaded, (A) 20,677lb (9379kg).

Performance: Maximum level speed at 36,000ft (11,000m) (A) Mach 1·4 (925mph, 1489km/h); (B) Mach 1·34; maximum rate of climb at S/L (A) 28,700ft/min (8750m/min); (B) 30,400ft/min (9265m/min); range with maximum fuel with reserve fuel for 20min maximum endurance at S/L (A) tanks retained 1,387 miles (2232km); (B) tanks retained 1,393 miles (2241km); range with tanks dropped (A) 1,612 miles (2594km), (B) 1,617 miles (2602km).

Armament: The Freedom Fighter has two Sidewinder missiles on wingtip launchers and two 20mm guns in the fuselage nose. Five pylons, one under the fuselage and two under each wing, enable the plane to carry a wide variety of loads. A bomb in excess of 2,000lb (910kg) or a high-rate-of-fire gun pack can be suspended from the center pylon.

History: First flight (A) May 1963; first flight production aircraft, October 1963; accepted into inventory January 1964. (B)—first flight, production aircraft 24 February 1964; operational service 30 April 1964.

Users: US Air Force; VNAF.

Below: Here dropping 2,000lb bombs, the F-5A has primitive bomb aiming by depressing the reticle of its lead-computing gunsight.

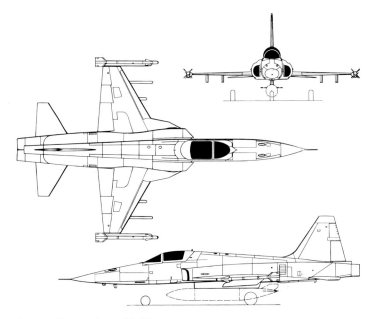

Above: Three-view of F-5A.

Tactical employment: The F-5 was developed as part of the US Military Assistance Program (MAP) to help allied nations update their tactical air forces. In 1965 the Air Force established an F-5 squadron at Williams Air Force Base, Arizona, for a test project in Southeast Asia. This project, as operation "Skoshi Tiger", entailed conducting a combat evaluation of the F-5 weapon system in Southeast Asia and collecting comparable data from similarly equipped aircraft (F-100 and F-4) operating in that theater. From ▶

▶October 1965 to March 1966, a squadron of 12 F-5 aircraft flew 2,659 combat sorties. Missions included close air support interdiction, escort, combat air patrol and armed reconnaissance, as the 4503rd Tactical Fighter Wing flew 2,500 hours over South Vietnam and Laos.

Though handicapped by small payload, the F-5 proved to be a worthwhile aircraft able to match some of the best capabilities of other fighters. Moreover its simplicity made it relatively easy to maintain and repair. Having demonstrated the F-5's usefulness, the men who had conducted the Skoshi Tiger evaluation now flew interdiction, armed reconnaissance and combat air patrols over North Vietnam.

The US Air Force began training the South Vietnamese Air Force with F-5 aircraft at Williams Air Force Base, Arizona, and in December 1966 the first VNAF crew returned to Vietnam where by the spring of 1967 they had flown hundreds of training sorties. Finally by June 1967, the Vietnamese were ready to fly their own combat sorties. At a formal ceremony held that same month at Bien Hoa the US Air Force officially turned the planes over to the South Vietnamese 522nd Fighter Squadron.

The United States Air Force continued to supply F-5s, including a few E models, to the South Vietnamese throughout the rest of the war and the aircraft remained a vital part of that country's air defense until the final collapse of the regime in 1975.

Below: One of the original F-5A Freedom Fighters in the Skoshi Tiger evaluation programme in 1965-66. Though obviously limited in capability, the F-5A proved to have excellent availability in Vietnam and spurred procurement by the USAF and USN of the F-5E.

Below: An F-5A of the VNAF (unit, 522nd Fighter Sqn) in 1967. In 1975 at least 1,100 US-built military aircraft were taken over by the Communist government of Vietnam, a few are still being used.

Above: Commun-
ist-captured
F-5B with
VPAF four-figure
serial numbers.
Apart from the
A-37 the F-5 was
the only Viet-
namese US-built
high-speed jet.

Right: F-5s be-
came operational
with the VNAF in
June 1967; this
one is at Bien Hoa.

Republic F-105 Thunderchief

F-105D, F, G.

Origin: Republic Aviation Division of Fairchild Hiller Corporation.
Type: (D) single-place, high performance, tactical fighter-bomber; (F) similar to D but with the fuselage extended to include a second seat, thus making it a fighter-bomber or trainer; (G) a modified Wild Weasel F-105F.
Engine: (D, F) one Pratt and Whitney J75-P-19W 25,000lb (12,030kg).
Dimensions: (F) span 34ft 11·2in (10·65m); length over all 69ft 1·18in (21·06m); length of fuselage 66ft 11·85in (20·42m); height over tail 20ft 1·96in (6·15m).
Weight: (F) Empty 28,393lb (12,879kg); maximum takeoff weight 54,000lb (24,495kg); maximum landing weight 51,038lb (23,150kg).
Performance: (F) Maximum speed at 38,000ft (11,600m) Mach 2·25; maximum speed at sea level Mach 1·25; maximum cruising speed Mach 0·95; range with maximum fuel 2,070 miles (3330km).
Armament: One General Electric M-61 20mm Vulcan automatic multi-barrel gun with 1,029 rounds. Sample loads include (a) 650gal centerline tank, 450gal tank on one inner wing pylon and two 3,000lb (360kg) bombs; (b) 650gal centerline tank and four GAM-83B Bullpup missiles; (c) three rocket packs on centreline, two on each inner wing pylon and one on each outer wing pylon.
History: First flight (D) 9 June 1959, (F) 11 June 1963; first acceptance (D) 28 September 1959, (F) 7 December 1963; entry to operational service (D) 1961, (F) 23 December 1963.
User: US Air Force, Tactical Air Command, PACAF.

Tactical employment: In early 1965 F-105Ds began flying combat strikes north of the 17th parallel. Thunderchiefs also performed tactical air strikes in South Vietnam and Laos. The F-105D made more strikes against North Vietnam than any other US aircraft and also suffered more losses.

Below: Tandem-seat F-105F engaged in dual-role combat mission with bomb load and white-painted Shrike anti-radar missiles.

Above: Three-view of F-105D (prior to Thunderstick-II mod).

The F-105Ds were consistently being modified to meet changing Southeast Asia combat needs. During the period 1965 to 1971 F-105Ds were equipped with armor plate, a secondary flight control system, and an improved pilot ejection seat. Other modifications included ECM pods for the wings and a more precise navigation system and better blind bombing capability for 30 F-105Ds.

Since it had the same basic failings as the D, the F underwent similar modifications to reduce vulnerability. Because it carried a second crewman the F model seemed well suited to the role of suppressing North Vietnam's missile defenses. Eighty-six F-105s fitted with radar homing and warning gear formed the backbone of the Wild Weasel program, initiated in 1965 to improve the US Air Force's electronic warfare capability. Upon pinpointing the radar at a missile site, the Wild Weasel attacked with Shrike missiles that homed on radar emissions. Thirteen of these modified Fs were sent to Southeast Asia in 1966 and 10 others soon followed. Fourteen of the 86▶

▶were modified to launch another antiradiation missile, the Standard ARM (AGM-78A/B) manufactured by General Dynamics for the US Navy.

The F-105G was a modified Wild Weasel F-105F which could protect itself by jamming enemy radar. This model used the Standard ARM rather than the older, shorter range Shrike.

As the war losses continued the aircraft was gradually phased out of USAF inventories, until by mid-1973 only 17 F-105Fs still flew, five with the Air Force and 12 with the US Air National Guard. However, 48 F-105Gs remained in the inventory. From 1965 to 1972 the aircraft performed yeoman service on many diversified missions in Southeast Asia. They had dropped bombs by day and occasionally by night from high or low altitude and, in their Wild Weasel guise, attacked SAM sites with their radar tracking air-to-ground missiles. During the war this versatile aircraft (F-105D) was also credited with 25 MiG kills.

Top: Because of its unique air inlets it was common to paint aircraft names (in this case *The Ripper*) on the outer side of the duct. This Thud flew with 355th TFW.

Above: One of the less-common items of ordnance in Vietnam, the AGM-12 Bullpup command-guided missile being fired by a Thunderchief in late October 1965 against a railroad bridge 110 miles (177km) north-west of Hanoi, causing severe damage.

Left: Bombing near Khe Sanh on Combat Sky-spot guidance from radar-equipped ground operators.

Sikorsky CH-54 Tarhe

CH-54A.

Origin: Sikorsky Aircraft, Div. of United Technologies Corp.
Type: Twin-turbine heavy flying crane helicopter.
Engines: Two 4,800shp Pratt & Whitney 773-1 turboshafts.
Dimensions: Main rotor diameter 72ft (21·95m); fuselage length 70ft 3in (21·41m).
Weight: Empty 19,234lb (8724kg); maximum takeoff 42,000lb (19,050kg).
Performance: (At normal takeoff weight of 38,000lb, 17,235kg) Maximum speed at sea level 126mph (203km/h); range with maximum fuel plus ten percent reserve 230 miles (370km).
Armament: None.
Accommodation: Three crew. With Universal Military pod can carry 45 troops, or 24 litters, maximum loaded weight 20,000lb (9072kg).
History: First flight 9 May 1962; first delivery in late 1964. On 28 June 1968 the Army accepted the Universal Military Pod for the CH-54.
User: US Army.

Tactical employment: The CH-54 was assigned to the US Army's 478th Aviation Company and performed outstanding service in support of the First Cavalry Division (Airmobile) in Southeast Asia. The Tarhe's use in airmobile operations included the transportation and positioning of heavy artillery and recovery of downed aircraft. On 29 April 1965 a CH-54 lifted 90 persons, including 87 combat equipped troops in a detachable van. Other Sky Cranes transported bulldozers and road graders weighing up to 17,500lb (7937kg) each and armoured vehicles of 20,000lb (9072kg), and

Right: A Tarhe carries a massive 10,000lb bomb (only the 15,000lb dropped by C-130s were larger) to clear a jungle area for a landing zone.

Below: CH-54A Tarhes retrieved more than 380 downed aircraft in Vietnam, worth $210 million. The largest was this C-123B, recovered in three instalments.

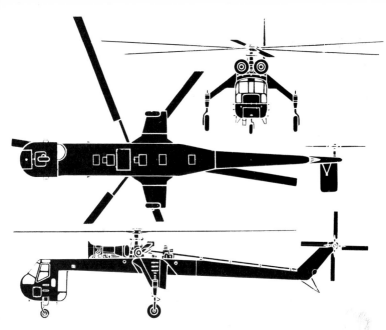

Above: Three-view of CH-54A distinguished by single main wheels.

other heavy hardware. They retrieved more than 380 damaged aircraft valued at $210 million.

Sikorsky H-34 Choctaw

H-34A, UH-34D Seahorse.

Origin: Sikorsky Aircraft Div., United Aircraft Corp.
Type: Single rotor transport helicopter.
Engines: One 1,525hp Wright R-1820-84C piston radial engine.
Dimensions: Main (4-bladed) rotor diameter 56ft (17·07m); fuselage length 46ft 9in (14·25m); height 14ft 3½in (4·36m).
Weight: Empty 7,650lb (3515kg); gross 13,000lb (5900kg).
Performance: Maximum speed at sea level 122mph (196km/h); cruising speed 97mph (156km/h); service ceiling 9,500ft (2900m); range with maximum fuel plus ten percent reserve 247 miles (400km).
Armament: None.
Accommodation: Two crew, 18 passengers, or 8 litters.
History: First flight 8 March 1954; deliveries to US Army began in April 1955.
Users: US Army (H-34A), USMC (UH-34D Seahorse), US Navy (SH-34).

Tactical employment: On 6 and 7 July 1964 the Viet Cong attacked the US Army Special Forces camp at Nam Dong in southwest Thua Thien province. Located at the junction of the borders of South and North Vietnam and Laos, the defenders had no tactical air support available. Their only hope lay in unarmed helicopters which would have to run the gauntlet of small arms fire to come to their aid. Eighteen Marine Corps helicopters and 10 Army H-34As met the challenge, delivering 9,500lb (431kg) of ammunition, medical supplies, and other equipment. After three ground assaults, the attackers were finally driven off. Special Forces Captain Roger H. C. Donlon was awarded the Congressional Medal of Honor for his bravery in this action.

The battle for Khe Sanh, from 20 January to 1 April 1968, was one of the most crucial and bitterly contested struggles of the Vietnam War. Throughout this long siege, the 26th Marines defended the base and positions on four hills (numbers 881, 861-A, 558 and 950) which dominated the strategic approaches into Northern I Corps. Opposed by two heavily armed and entrenched North Vietnamese Army divisions, the Americans held out and denied the communists victory.

The Americans' success was due in large part to a massive airlift. Among

Below: Departure of UH-34D Seahorses from USS *Princeton* taking Marines to embattled Rung Sa area on 26 March 1966.

Above: Three-view of UH-34 (all H-34 models basically similar).

the transport aircraft which participated were UH-34Ds of Marine Aircraft Group (MAG)-36. The helicopters flew in and out of Khe Sanh daily delivering supplies, cargo, reinforcements, and evacuating casualties. Flying from Quang Tri and Dong Ha, the UH-34 pilots braved low ceilings and enemy ground fire to help sustain the defenders of Khe Sanh. During February as monsoon clouds rolled into the valley, the North Vietnamese emplaced heavy automatic weapons along the peaks neighboring the American mountain outposts. They waited for the ceiling to clear and the arrival of the American helicopters. As a result, the UH-34s, CH-46s, and UH-1Es were subjected to a murderous barrage during each mission.

Below: Marines going aboard UH-34 helicopters at the conclusion of Operation Essex on 9 November 1967.

Sikorsky CH-53 Sea Stallion

CH-53A; HH-53B Super Jolly Green Giant

Origin: Sikorsky Aircraft Div., United Technologies Corp.
Type: Twin-turbine heavy assault transport helicopter.
Engines: Two 2,850shp General Electric T64-GE-6 turboshafts.
Dimensions: Main (6-blade) rotor diameter 72ft 3in (22·02m); fuselage length 67ft 2in (20·47m).
Weight: Empty 22,444lb (10,180kg); maximum takeoff (HH-53B) 42,000lb (19,050kg).
Performance: (HH-53B) Maximum level speed at sea level 186mph (299km/h); range with 9,926lb (4502kg) fuel and two auxiliary 450 gallon (1703 litre) tanks, plus ten percent reserve 540 miles (869km).
Armament: (HH-53B) Three 7·62mm miniguns.
Accommodation: Three crew, 37 troops, or 24 litters and 4 attendants.
History: (CH-53A) First flight 14 October 1964; deliveries began in mid-1966. (HH-53B) First flight 15 March 1967; deliveries began in June 1967.
Users: US Marine Corps (CH-53A); US Air Force (HH-53B).

Tactical employment: Altogether the HH-53 was the largest, fastest and most powerful heavy lift helicopter in the US Air Force inventory. Adapted from a US Marine Corps helicopter, the HH-53B began to fly combat

Above: Heavier than it looks, a trailer of drinking water is airlifted in to Hill 119 Marines by a CH-53A; limit load 10 tons.

Above right: CH-53D countermeasures helicopter of Navy squadron HM-12 (based on USS *Dubuque*) tows the Mk 105 magnetic mine-sweeping device across Haiphong harbour, 1973.

Right: An HH-53C Super Jolly of the USAF 40th Aerospace Rescue & Recovery Sqn over Vietnam in 1968. The HH-53C introduced the 3,435hp T64-7 engine as well as long-range tanks and FR probe.

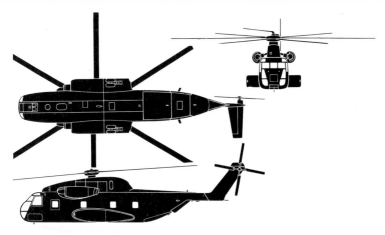

Above: Three-view of CH-53A Sea Stallion.

missions in late 1967. Also in 1967 the US Air Force started a three-year development program to acquire a night rescue capability. By March 1971 it had succeeded in installing a nighttime recovery system aboard five HH-53C helicopters in Southeast Asia.

One of the greatest allies of the Viet Cong and the North Vietnamese was ▶

▶ the cover of darkness. Various devices were tried in an effort to pierce the dark including the mounting of searchlights and infrared equipment on helicopters. However, because the helicopters' noise warned the enemy of their approach, the experiment was discarded and assigned to quieter fixed-wing aircraft.

The HH-53, with several support aircraft, played a key role in the dramatic, but unsuccessful attempt to rescue the American prisoners of war held in the Son Tay prison compound, near Hanoi, on 20/21 November 1970.

Another well-known operation, involving this time the CH-53 variant, concerned the Cambodian seizure of the American merchantship the *Mayaguez* on 12 May 1975, which brought a swift and strong response. Part of the assault operation to free the ship's crew included a helicopter force of CH-53s, one of which crashed because of mechanical failure, killing all 23 personnel on board. Before dawn on 15 May eight CH-53s took off from U Tapao intending to attack two landing zones on Koh Tang, the island off Cambodia where the crew was believed held. However, the island was garrisoned by Cambodians who shot down or badly damaged five helicopters. Since the ship's crew was thought to have been somewhere on Koh Tang, no air or naval prelanding strikes had been made. Eventually, three CH-53s landed their troops on the island and three more helicopters landed Marines on the destroyer escort USS *Holt* from which they boarded the *Mayaguez*.

Right: Picking up an A-4E Skyhawk at Da Nang for shipment to Iwakuni, Japan, for overhaul; CH-53A from Marine Air Group 12.

Below: A Marine and a wet-suited Air Force para-rescueman sprint for an Air Force HH-53C during the rescue of the *Mayaguez* from Cambodian forces on 15 May 1975.

Sikorsky HH-3

HH-3 and SH-3D Sea King; HH-3E Jolly Green Giant.

Origin: Sikorsky Aircraft Div., United Technologies Corp.
Engines: Two 1,400shp General Electric T58-GE-10 turboshafts.
Type: Twin-engined, all-weather search and rescue helicopter.
Dimensions: Main (five-blade) rotor diameter 62ft (18·90m); fuselage length 54ft 9in (16·69m).
Weights: Empty (simple transport versions, typical) 9,763lb (4428kg); maximum loaded (transport) usually 21,500lb (9750kg).
Performance: Maximum level speed at 20,500lb (9300kg) 166mph (267km/h); range with maximum fuel plus ten percent reserve 625 miles (1005km).
Armament: Provision for 840lb (381kg) of weapons, including torpedoes.
Accommodation: Crew of four, 25 to 30 troops, or 15 litters, or 5,000lb (2270kg) of cargo.
History: First flight 11 March 1959; first SH-3D delivered in June 1966. (HH-3E) first flight of Jolly Green Giant 17 June 1963. On 31 May–1 June 1967 two HH-3Es made the first non-stop transatlantic flights by helicopter from New York to the Paris Air Show. Each aircraft made nine mid-air refuelings.
Users: US Navy (HH-3 and SH-3D); US Air Force, Air Rescue Service (HH-3E).

Tactical employment: In July 1965 the Tactical Air Command (TAC) loaned the Air Rescue Service two CH-3 cargo helicopters. The CH-3 was specially modified for rescue operations and designated the HH-3. The new helicopters, the HH-3E and its less powerful companion the HH-3C, quickly acquired the nickname Jolly Green Giant. In terms of speed, endurance, and ceiling the HH-3 resembled the CH-3, but the former carried auxiliary fuel tanks which extended its range to 625 miles. Operating out of Udorn, or Da Nang, the Jolly Green Giant could fly to any point in North Vietnam and return home. ▶

Below: From this angle the full-width rear door and ramp can be seen, as well as the lowered tricycle landing gear (HH-3C).

Above: Three-view of HH-3 series (nosewheel gear and rear doors).

Above: HC-130P tanker's view of an HH-3E Jolly Green Giant as it noses in for an aerial refueling off the coast of Vietnam, late 1967.

►   The HH-3E carried communications equipment which was compatible with other friendly aircraft operating in Southeast Asia. It also possessed an external variable-speed hoist with a 240-foot (73m) long cable stressed to lift 600-pound (272kg) loads. The HH-3Es still lacked the full capacity to loiter for long periods over enemy territory. Upon recommendation of the Air Rescue Service, Air Force Systems Command (AFSC) developed and tested mid-air refuelings by HC-130P aircraft of the HH-3E. Adopted in 1967, the HC-130P/HH-3E combination demonstrated an eight-hour mission. The HC-130P/HH-3E then began flying daily operations. By January approximately 525 H-3 helicopters had been delivered to the military services.

Above: Vietnamese troops escort a Viet Cong prisoner from a CH-3C delivered to a South Vietnam base at Nha Trang, April 1966.

Left: Loading Igloo White Spikebuoy sensors from a trailer into a more powerful CH-3E at Nakhon Phanom RTAFB in June 1968.

Below: A fine portrait of an HH-3E on a jungle rescue mission. On many USAF aircraft the tan colour had a pinkish hue.

Vought A-7 Corsair II

A-7A, D, E.

Origin: Vought Systems Division of LTV.
Type: Single-seat attack plane.
Engine: (A) one 11,350lb (5150kg) thrust Pratt and Whitney TF30-6 two-shaft turbofan; (D) 14,250lb (6465kg) Allison TF41-1 (Rolls-Royce Spey derivative) of same layout: (E) 15,000lb (6804kg) TF41-2.
Dimensions: Wing span 38ft 9in (11·08m); length 46ft 1½in (14·06m); height 16ft ¾in (4·90m).
Weights: Empty (A) 15,904lb (7214kg); (D) 19,781lb (8972kg); maximum loaded (A) 32,500lb (14,750kg); (D) 42,000lb (19,050kg).
Performance: Maximum level speed at sea level 606 knots (698mph, 1123km/h); maximum level speed at 5,000ft (1525m) with 12 Mk 82 bombs 562 knots (646mph, 1040km/h); tactical radius with weapon load typically 715 miles (1150km); ferry range with four external tanks approximately 4,100 miles (6600km).
Armament: (A) two 20mm Colt MK 12 in nose; six wing and two fuselage pylons for weapon load of 15,000lb (6804kg); (D, E) one 20mm M61 Vulcan cannon on left side of fuselage with 1,000-round drum; external load up to theoretical 20,000lb (9072kg). Weapons carried include air-to-air and air-to-ground missiles; general purpose bombs; rockets; gunpods; and auxiliary fuel tanks.
History: First flight (A) 27 September 1965, (D) 5 April 1968, (E) 25 November 1968; first deliveries to user squadrons (A) 14 October 1966; first combat (A) 3 December 1967.
Users: US Navy and Air Force.

Tactical employment: In the early 1960s the Navy began searching for a subsonic attack plane able to carry a greater load of non-nuclear weapons than the A-4E Skyhawk. Ling Temco Vought entered the competition, and to keep costs low based its entry on the F-8 Crusader. The strategy apparently worked, for in 1964 the Navy selected the LTV Aerospace Corporation the winner of a design competition.

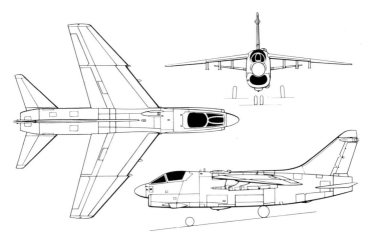

Above: Three-view of A-7D Corsair II (A-7E almost identical).

The Navy's A-7A saw its first action during December 1967, after being launched from carriers on the Gulf of Tonkin. Delivery of 199 A-7As was completed the following spring. The A-7B, a version of the A but powered with a more powerful engine entered combat in Vietnam on 4 March 1969.

The A-7D was the tactical fighter version used by the United States Air Force. It was equipped with a continuous-solution navigation and weapon delivery system, and could bomb accurately by radar, regardless of the weather. The first Air Force unit equipped with the A-7D was the 54th Tactical Fighter Wing at Luke Air Force Base, Arizona. The A-7D entered combat in Southeast Asia in October 1972, flown by the 354th Tactical Fighter Wing which deployed from Myrtle Beach Air Force Base, South Carolina.

The A-7E, later redesignated the C, served the US Navy as a light attack, close air support, and interdiction aircraft. It entered into combat in Southeast Asia with attack squadrons 146 and 147 in May 1970.

In the fall of 1972, in reaction to the previous summer's southward advance of the North Vietnamese, the US Air Force used the A-7D for the first time against parts of the Ho Chi Minh Trail and for close air support of friendly Lao units. During Linebacker II operations (December 1972 to January 1973) the USAF used the A-7D as a strike aircraft for daylight tactical missions. During these strikes F-4 Pathfinders navigated and designated targets for delivery of unguided bombs by other F-4s and the A-7s. In May 1973 the Air Force used the A-7D extensively in repeated strikes against the Khmer Rouge insurgents attacking the Cambodian Capital of Phnom Penh. An Air Force A-7D piloted by Capt. Lonnie O. Ratley flew the last strike of the Southeast Asian war, bombing a target in Cambodia on 15 August 1973.

Left: Strop attached, an A-7A is readied for cat launch from USS _Constellation_ in late 1968, with self-defence Sidewinder AAMs.

An A-7E from VA-147, also flying from _Constellation_ in late 1972.

Vought F-8

RF-8A, G, F-8E, H.

Origin: Vought Systems Division of LTV.

Type: Single-place carrier-based day fighter. RF-8A is the photographic version of the F-8A. The RF-8G has additional cameras and navigationa' and electronic equipment.

Engine: (A) one Pratt and Whitney J57-P-4A two-shaft turbojet with afterburner 16,000lb (7327kg); (D, E, G, H) J57-P-20A or -22, 18,000lb (8165kg).

Dimensions: Span (A) 35ft 8in (10·87m); length overall 54ft 3in (16·54m); height 15ft 9in (4·80m).

Weights: Normal takeoff weight (F-8C) 27,500lb (12,500kg); maximum takeoff weight (F-8E/J) 34,000lb (15,420kg).

Performance: Maximum speed clean at altitude (A) 1,013mph (1688km/h); (RF-8A) 982mph (1636km/h), (RF-8G) 1,002mph (1661 km/h); initial climb (typical) 21,000ft/min (6400m/min); combat radius (F-8A) 600 miles (965km).

Armament: (A) four 20mm Colt MK 12 cannot with 84 rounds; one side-winder on each side and 32 folding fin rockets in belly pack; 2,000lb (906kg) bombs (see Tactical employment).

History: First flight (production F-8A) November 1956, (RF-8A) 17 December 1956.

Users: US Navy and US Marine Corps.

Tactical employment: The F-8 first saw action early in America's involve-ment in the Southeast Asian conflict. In May of 1964 RF-8As performed photo reconnaissance missions over communist controlled areas. F-8s also participated in the first Gulf of Tonkin reprisal attacks against North Vietnam in August 1964. They were also used in the myriad attacks against North Vietnam (Rolling Thunder) including the April 1965 strike against the Thanh Hoa Bridge. That same spring F-8s participated in the first night armed reconnaissance mission of the war.

The Navy did not have a monopoly on F-8s in Southeast Asia as Marine RF-8As were active in that theater from the spring of 1964. Since Marine infantry had trained with their own and Navy tactical squadrons, they made effective use of close air support. General Westmoreland was so impressed with Marine and Navy tactical air that he requested semi-permanent carrier assignments off South Vietnam.

Above right: The F-8 Crusader did much work in Vietnam in the ground attack role. Here an F-8E fires 3in rockets in March 1966.

Left: Flying in close support of Marines, an F-8E from VMF(AW)-312 overflies a bomb explosion.

The F-8 Crusader represented half or more of the carrier fighters in the Tonkin Gulf of the first four years of the war. The Navy's Crusader under Commander Jim Stockdale, later POW and Medal of Honor winner, made first use of 2,000lb (906kg) bombs on the F-8. His innovation required a catapult launch with a minimum of fuel to reduce takeoff weight. When airborne the aircraft refueled from an aerial tanker.

The Crusader sometimes played the role of decoy in the battle against the SAMs. In 1966 the Navy was convinced that enemy radar operators could not differentiate among the types of planes on their screen, so it decided to send a two plane section above and ahead of the strike force. This was done to get the radar-controlled SAM battery to concentrate on the first and clearest target, thereby allowing the attacking divisions to reach their targets at little or no risk. For this type of mission the F-8s carried no external munitions to attain better maneuverability and airspeed in dodging SAMs that were launched. On many such missions the enemy fired in excess of eight SAMs forcing the Crusader pilots to conjure-up their best aviation skills to avoid the glowing doom. The tactic worked, as on many occasions the strike planes made it to their targets without enduring a single SAM loss.

When fighting MiGs, the F-8 either escorted strike and reconnaissance aircraft or patrolled assigned sectors in hope of engaging MiGs enroute to intercepting US formations. Photo escort missions generally involved one fighter covering an RF-8. On these missions the reconnaissance aircraft usually flew at 4,000ft (1220m) above the ground with the fighter situated at four o'clock. This mission was the most dangerous and the most costly for the camera-equipped Crusader. Indeed, the Navy's photosquadrons endured a loss rate three times the Navy's average because the RF-8 had to fly straight and constant courses to achieve the best results, making the aircraft vulnerable to anti-aircraft fire. Twenty RF-8Gs were lost during the war, which was nearly a quarter of the total Crusader losses. During the period 1968 to 1971 such photo-reconnaissance flights represented the majority of the US flights over North Vietnam.

The combat attrition rate of the F-8 was comparable to similar fighters. From 1964 to 1973 83 Crusaders were either lost or destroyed by enemy fire. Another 109 aircraft needed major rebuilding.

The Crusader is credited with shooting down 19 MiGs in Vietnam and the majority of those were downed with the AIM-9 missile. For the period 1965–1968 the Crusader dominated the carriers' air combat statistics. During that time carrier air wings accounted for 34 MiG kills with Phantoms claiming 13 while A-1s and A-4s claimed three. Thus, the Crusader was credited with nearly 53 per cent of the MiG kills.

OTHER SUPER-VALUE MILITARY GUIDES IN THIS SERIES......

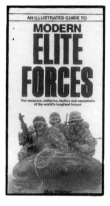

Aircraft Markings
Allied Fighters of World War II
Battleships and Battlecruisers
Bombers of World War II
German, Italian and Japanese Fighters
 of World War II
Israeli Air Force
Military Helicopters
Modern Airborne Missiles
Modern Destroyers
Modern Fighters and Attack Aircraft
Modern Soviet Air Force
Modern Soviet Ground Forces

Modern Soviet Navy
Modern Sub Hunters
Modern Submarines
Modern Tanks
Modern US Air Force
Modern US Army
Modern US Navy
Modern Warships
NATO Fighters
Pistols and Revolvers
Rifles and Sub-machine Guns
Space Warfare
World War II Tanks

✱Each has 160 fact-filled pages
✱Each is colourfully illustrated with hundreds of action photos and technical drawings
✱Each contains concisely presented data and accurate descriptions of major international weapons
✱Each represents tremendous value

If you would like further information on any of our titles please write to:
Publicity Dept. (Military Div.), Salamander Books Ltd.,
52 Bedford Row, London WC1R 4LR

PRINTED IN BELGIUM BY
proost
INTERNATIONAL BOOK PRODUCTION